Stadium Stories:
Missouri Tigers

Stadium Stories™ Series

Stadium Stories:
Missouri Tigers

Brian C. Peterson

INSIDERS' GUIDE®

GUILFORD, CONNECTICUT
AN IMPRINT OF THE GLOBE PEQUOT PRESS

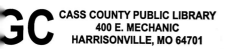

INSIDERS' GUIDE®

Text design: Casey Shain

All photos are courtesy of University of Missouri Athletic Media Relations, except where noted.
Cover photos: *front cover:* Brad Smith (Newman Lawrence); *back cover:* top, Dan Devine and Don Faurot; bottom, Missouri Tiger statue.

Library of Congress Cataloging-in-Publication Data
Peterson, Brian C.
    Stadium stories: Missouri Tigers / Brian Peterson.–1st ed.
        p. cm. – (Stadium stories series)
    ISBN 0-7627-3820-0
    1. University of Missouri–Football–History. 2. Missouri Tigers (Football team)–History. I. Title: Missouri Tigers. II. Title III. Series.

GV958.U5294P48 2005
796.332'63'0977829–dc22   2005047644

Manufactured in the United States of America
First Edition/First Printing

Contents

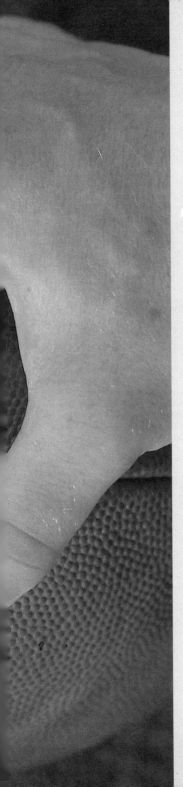

The Mystique of Mizzou

There is something very special about football at Ol' Mizzou. It is something so unique that you have to experience it to truly understand its depths. Missouri football is not about the number of national championships the team has won (the highest the Tigers ever finished in the polls was fourth in 1960) or how many Heisman Trophy winners it has produced (the answer is none, although "Pitchin' Paul" Christman finished third behind Iowa's Nile Kinnick and Michigan's Tom Harmon for the award in 1939). Instead, Tiger football's greatness lies in its rugged authenticity.

Missouri's black and gold uniform is worn by young men raised in close-knit families from Norman Rockwell towns. Love for the Tigers is a fundamental, raw emotion that springs from the same well that instills a sense of duty in a U.S. Marine, the zeal of an evangelical minister, or the willingness of a farmer to get up before dawn to till the land.

"I think what separates Missourians from the rest of the country is the ability to rebound," said 1945 Mizzou graduate Hugh Stephenson, Jr., a former president of the school's board of curators and medical chief of staff at the university's hospital and medical center. "No matter what life seems to throw at Missouri folks, they never seem to give in. They are tremendously resilient, unwavering in their determination. Even in down years, Missouri fans fill the stadium to stand behind their boys."

Tiger football is not about glitz and glamour. It is all about effort, perseverance, and attitude.

"What separates MU football fans is their loyalty regardless of the team's performance," said Andy Ekern, Tigers tackle and team captain in 1982. "And these fans aren't just loyal, they're extremely knowledgeable. I've lived in Chicago for the past twenty years and Wrigley fans are enthusiastic, but I can't say that they truly understand the history of the Cubs. Mizzou fans remember all of the history and use that to set the standards for the current era."

My passion for Missouri football comes honestly. I bled black and gold in the mid-1980s, when those colors were not fashionable.

The Tiger paws that line the Stadium Boulevard exit off Interstate 70, the Golden Girls, and the massive columns in front of Jesse Hall provided an inspirational setting. But the 1980s were not good to Missouri football on the field.

That didn't stop me from falling in love with the stately school the first time I stepped into the athletic administration offices as a high school senior (during a self-made recruiting trip from California). With game films in hand, I went over my strengths, weaknesses, and dreams with a Tigers assistant coach.

Instead of attending Missouri directly out of high school, I accepted a football scholarship at Azusa Pacific University in my home state of California. But I never got Missouri out of my heart. After my second football season at APU, I transferred to Mizzou and walked on the Tigers' football team during the spring semester of 1987.

I spent a glorious three months learning a new position (cornerback), making tackles on the awful OmniTurf of Faurot Field, running from the dorm to the weight room in the early morning, and participating in the annual Black and Gold game.

The University of Missouri's top-ranked journalism school was the main reason for my decision to move to Columbia. Before the 1987 college season, I left the playing field for the press box.

I will never forget my cup of coffee with Tiger football, though. Whether you are a walk-on or one of the nation's top high school recruits, the University of Missouri draws you in and refuses to let you go.

Founded in 1839, the University of Missouri was the first publicly supported institution of higher learning established in the Louisiana Territory. The school is located smack-dab in the

The University of Missouri's six columns, which tower in front of Jesse Hall, are all that remain of the orginal Academic Hall.

middle of the state in Columbia, Missouri—two hours east of St. Louis and two hours west of Kansas City along Interstate 70.

Since the early 1990s *Money* magazine has consistently ranked Columbia among the top places to live in its annual "Best Places to Live" survey. The historic Katy Trail runs through Columbia, and the university's schools of journalism, engineering, and agriculture are among the nation's best.

With state-of-the-art health care facilities, quick access to the state capital in Jefferson City and beautiful vacation resorts at the Lake of the Ozarks, and a low cost of living, Columbia is a very attractive place to live. However, if you're an opponent of the Missouri Tigers football team, visiting Columbia can be a nightmare.

Famous Mizzou Alumni

Tom Berenger, actor
Linda Bloodworth-Thomason, screenwriter/producer
Kate Capshaw, actress
Sheryl Crow, singer
Eugene Field, author
Harold S. Hook, businessman
Stan Kroenke, businessman
James Lehrer, television broadcaster
Robert Loggia, actor
Marlin Perkins, television host
Brad Pitt, actor
Dick Richards, NASA astronaut
Debbye Turner, Miss America 1990
Elizabeth Vargas, television broadcaster
Sam Walton, businessman
Tennessee Williams, playwright

Throughout its history, Columbia hasn't been very hospitable to visiting schools. Some of Missouri's greatest upsets have come within the confines of Memorial Stadium, including the Tigers' 20–14 victory over Southern Methodist University in 1948.

The game against fourth-ranked SMU helped Missouri establish a reputation as a giant killer at home. Subsequent upsets at Memorial Stadium included a 20–17 defeat of seventh-ranked Colorado in 1972, a 13–12 victory over second-ranked Nebraska in 1973, a 9–0 decision over Arizona State in 1974, and a 19–14 conquest of fifteenth-ranked Oklahoma in 1981.

SMU entered the 1948 contest on a fifteen-game winning streak, with designs on a national championship and featuring All-America back Doak Walker, who would win the Heisman Trophy that year. The Tigers were unranked and coming off a mediocre 6–4 season in 1947.

The Mustangs expected to go unbeaten in 1948. Walker had made the cover of *Life* magazine. A then record crowd of nearly 31,000 showed up at Memorial Stadium to see if Missouri, which had lost to SMU 17–0 and 35–19 the previous two years, could pull off a shocker.

"Nobody expected us to win, but we got the upset," John Kadlec, a guard on the 1948 Tigers team, told the *Columbia Missourian*. "It was a big ball game, that's for sure."

After a scoreless first quarter, Walker intercepted a pass and on the ensuing drive helped the Mustangs advance 50 yards down the field, culminating with his 1-yard touchdown run. Missouri tied the game at 7–7 by marching 70 yards on the first drive of the second half. Gus Entsminger, considered by many the best Split T formation quarterback Don Faurot ever coached with the Tigers, ran 7 yards for the game-tying score.

Midway through the third quarter, the Mustangs had moved the ball to Missouri's 10 yard line. However, fullback Dick McKissack fumbled the ball, and Tigers linebacker Win Carter recovered. Entsminger followed the fumble recovery with a 59-yard run.

Mizzou eventually moved the ball to SMU's 2 yard line, but SMU stopped the Tigers there on four downs. Following a Mustangs punt, Missouri scored on halfback Dick Braznell's short sweep around end to take a 14–7 lead.

With four minutes remaining in the fourth quarter, Missouri's Loyd Brinkman intercepted a Mustangs pass and returned it 49 yards to SMU's 5 yard line. Johnny Glorioso ran it into the end zone, and the Tigers led 20–7.

Walker concluded the scoring with an impressive 55-yard touchdown reception, but it was too little too late. The Tigers outgained the Mustangs 365 rushing yards to 84 in the improbable win.

"Faurot had done a lot of great things during his tenure, including improving the school's financial picture," said former Tigers head coach Dan Devine in his autobiography, *Simply Devine*. "The big break came in 1948, when the Tigers beat SMU and Heisman Trophy winner Doak Walker. The game is still remembered as one of the best in school history."

Another of the school's most memorable games came in 1911—and it started a tradition that continues to this day.

Things were not good at Missouri at the time. Something had to be done to remedy the situation. Only the support of the Mizzou family could make things better . . .

Those thoughts may have been going through the mind of Chester L. Brewer as he took over as Missouri's athletic director and football coach in 1911. By that year the Tigers had defeated archrival Kansas just four times in the first twenty years of their rivalry.

Losing anything to Kansas is unacceptable to the people of the Show-Me State. To make matters worse, the Jayhawks had shut out Ol' Mizzou in half of their fourteen victories. (Two of the games had ended in ties.)

Each of the rivalry's initial twenty games had been played on neutral sites in Kansas City. However, in 1911 the rules in college football changed, and schools were required to play all of their games on campus.

Brewer found just what he needed to stop the mounting losses to Kansas and to generate revenue to help Missouri build new bleachers at Rollins Field (where the Tigers played before the building of Memorial Stadium in 1926). In a stroke of genius, he called on University of Missouri alums from all over the country to return home for the big game.

Throughout the week before the game, the *Columbia Missourian* listed the names of everyone who planned on coming to Columbia. "Beat Kansas" sales were the rage at local stores. Alumni attended dinners in their honor, fans organized pep rallies, and a parade and bonfire provided additional pomp and circumstance. An estimated 1,600 people traveled to Columbia, and more than 9,000 filled Rollins Field for the game.

The Tigers didn't disappoint their faithful. Both teams had tough, stingy defenses, and the Jayhawks took a 3–0 lead late into the game. Mizzou tied the score when captain Glen Shuck kicked a game-tying field goal with less than four minutes remaining.

Missouri's Billy Blees protected the tie by tackling a Kansas runner from behind as he raced toward a possible game-winning touchdown in the final seconds. Tiger fans carried Blees off the field on their shoulders after the play.

That 3–3 tie game between Mizzou and Kansas began the tradition of college Homecomings throughout the country. (The University of Illinois also claims to have started the Homecoming tradition.)

The Homecoming game raised an estimated $20,000 to help Missouri improve its athletic facilities. More importantly, it changed the tide of the rivalry with the Jayhawks. The Tigers hold an 18–7–2 record against Kansas in Homecoming games.

Overall Missouri is 52–35–2 in Homecoming games, but from 1961 to 1999 the Tigers did not face the Jayhawks in that annual game. The teams resumed their Homecoming battles in 2000, with Kansas stealing a 38–17 victory. Missouri returned the favor with a 36–12 pounding in 2002.

Homecoming at Mizzou has always been more than just a game. The school held its first Homecoming dance in 1928 and crowned its first Homecoming queen in 1932. In 1935 sororities and fraternities started a tradition of creating massive decorations called "house decks" on the front of their houses. By the 1940s the freshmen formed a pep club called the "Thundering Thousand" that marched from the columns to the stadium. In the fifties, students organized pep rallies called "Romp, Stomp, and Chomp."

In 1931 three students lit the bonfire the night before the school pep rally. Approximately one hundred students worked through the night to rebuild the pile. All male students were let out of class early the next day to help finish the job. And for a brief time Mizzou students tried a nightshirt parade. The team, coaches, and the Homecoming queen and her court all wore nightshirts in the parade and at the pep rally.

One year the school newspaper, *The Missouri Student*, backed "Operation Mascot," an effort to find a live Tiger mascot. The cost of getting a live mascot for Homecoming would have been about $2,500, including the price of the tiger, food, a cage, and transportation. The New York Zoological Society ended the

Through good times and tough times, Missouri fans have remained steadfast in their support of Tiger football.

campaign when it wrote a letter to the University of Missouri saying tiger cubs were unsuitable to use as mascots.

World events have occasionally had an impact on the Homecoming celebration. Missouri canceled its Homecoming in 1918 due to the great influenza epidemic known as the Spanish Flu. In 1944 the Homecoming game against the University of Kansas was moved to Kansas City to save gasoline for the war effort.

For nearly a century, Homecoming has brought the entire Mizzou family together. In fact, family is a recurring theme in the history of Tiger football.

Fighting Tigers

The bomb. The shotgun. The blitz. Football has incorporated a lot of terminology and symbolism from warfare into its fabric. At the University of Missouri, you can add the Tigers fight song, "Every True Son," to that list.

Composer Fred Waring used an adaptation of the World War I marching tune "It's a Long Way to Tipperary" as the basis for "Every True Son" in 1946. Until that year, the only fight song Mizzou played was "Dixie." Another fight song, which replaced "Dixie" in the 1960s, was "Fight Tiger." Here are the lyrics to "Fight Tiger":

> *Fight, Tiger, fight for old Mizzou,*
> *Right behind you, everyone is with you,*
> *Break the line and follow down the field,*
> *And you'll be, on the top, upon the top.*
> *Fight, Tiger, you will always win,*
> *Proudly keep the colors flying skyward.*
> *In the end, we'll win the victory,*
> *So Tigers fight for Old Mizzou!*

Ol' Mizzou also got its Tigers nickname from wartime experiences. During the Civil War, the citizens of Columbia formed a militia to defend the town from guerillas, raiders, and marauders. In 1864 the Columbia militia began to disband; a new guard called the Missouri Tigers formed shortly afterward, and the city of Columbia was never attacked. To honor the original Tigers, the University of Missouri athletic committee named its teams after them in 1890.

If you want to fathom how deep the love for Missouri football flows, spend some time talking with the Ekern family. Raised approximately thirty miles northeast of Columbia in the small town of Mexico, Missouri, the Ekern boys—Bert, Bill, Pete, George, and Carol—have all worn the black and gold uniform. Bill's son Bill, Jr., played freshman ball at MU, and Pete's sons Andy, a tackle, and Kirk, a linebacker, both made the varsity.

"What makes Missouri so special is that it's so family oriented," Pete said. "The people of Missouri are very close to the university. The fans turn out whether MU goes 10–1 or 1–10. It also adds to the atmosphere that most of the players stay in Missouri after their college days."

Bert, the eldest Ekern brother, was an All–Big Six end for the Tigers in 1942. His 77-yard touchdown reception from Bob Steuber set a school record and helped the Tigers defeat Iowa State 39–13 in 1941. It was one of the few passing plays Mizzou actually ran during the year head coach Don Faurot unveiled his vaunted Split T formation.

The Tigers won twenty-two games and two Big Six Conference championships during Bert's career. In 1941 Mizzou lost 2–0 to Fordham in the Sugar Bowl.

"We were just a bunch of boys having a whole lot of fun back then," Bert said. "We were tickled to have games because our practices were tougher than the games."

According to Bert, he and Bill first honed their football skills as part of a grade school team named the Rattlesnakes. The Rattlesnakes were made up of twelve or thirteen local Mexico boys who wore sweatshirts and sneakers in exhibitions against the Missouri Military Academy, also located in Mexico. Bill remem-

Odds and Ends

Missouri's first mascot was a bulldog named Grover Cleveland. Today it's Truman the Tiger, named in 1984 after Missouri native and U.S. President Harry S Truman. Truman the Tiger has been recognized as the "Best Mascot in the Nation" in national competitions.

In 1999 *Sports Illustrated* ranked the fifty greatest sports figures in Missouri history. Number 11 on the list is cornerback Roger Wehrli, number 21 is linebacker Andy Russell, number 31 is Don Faurot, and number 38 is "Pitchin' Paul" Christman. Obviously, *SI* should have put Faurot number one—and where was Dan Devine?

Fittingly, Missouri's 500th victory came in a 31–21 victory over Kansas in 1990—the one-hundredth anniversary of Tigers football.

In 1927 the Tigers asked Nebraska for ideas for a trophy to be given to the winner of their annual game. The Cornhuskers suggested a bell that two fraternities on the Lincoln, Nebraska, campus had battled for in various academic and athletic contests. Missouri agreed. The bell has an M on one side and an N on the other.

Mizzou athletic director Chester Brewer and members of a secret honorary society, the Mystical Seven, began the tradition of the Tiger-Sooner Peace Pipe in 1929. The Mystical Seven and a similar group from Oklahoma perform the smoking of the peace pipe ceremony at halftime of the annual game.

Just before the 1959 game at Iowa State, Mizzou assistant coaches put on their headsets and shortly realized they could hear the Cyclones' coaches. The wire mix-up led Northwestern Bell of Ames to donate a Telephone Trophy to the winner of the Iowa State–Missouri game each year since.

The Tigers won the inaugural games for the Missouri-Nebraska Bell, the Tiger-Sooner Peace Pipe, and the Telephone Trophy.

bered that the Rattlesnakes scrimmaged the academy during halftime of a few Tigers games in the mid-thirties.

At Mexico High School, Bill played in an offense similar to what the University of Michigan was running at the time. He was a fullback who received the direct snap. During his sophomore year at Mizzou, there were three players ahead of him on the depth chart, so he switched to guard and end to get playing time. On the B-team, he was first-string quarterback and second-string running back.

"I fondly remember having the opportunity to play a variety of positions," said Bill, who would not have attended Missouri if it were not for the upstanding character of—and a promise from—Faurot. All the Ekern boys were excellent students, and Bill originally had his sights set on the Naval Academy. To get Bill to Mizzou, Faurot promised to help Bill get an appointment to the Academy after two seasons if he didn't like the Tigers' program.

While Bert never lost to Kansas in three seasons, Bill was not as fortunate. In his senior year, Bill scored the only touchdown in the game against the Jayhawks, but the Tigers were penalized on the point-after attempt that would have tied the game at 7–7. Mizzou failed on the subsequent PAT and lost the game 7–6.

"The week before the Kansas game, my dad became furious when the *Kansas City Star* ran a picture of Bert with a caption that said they expected him to be the star of the game," said Bill. "At the time, Bert was in the South Pacific in a submarine serving in World War II. The paper may have mixed me and Bert up before the game, but I made sure they got the right Ekern in the paper after the game."

Bill graduated from the University of Missouri in only three years with an engineering degree. Following his final football season in 1943, Bill was invited to play in the annual game between the College All-Stars and the NFL champion. However, he had to write a letter turning down the invitation when the dean of the engineering school would not allow him to miss class time to play.

Pete was the next Ekern to play for Mizzou. He was followed by George, who played at the junior varsity level, and Carol, who, after returning from the army, played one season of freshman ball before being called back into military service.

Like Bert, Pete, who played for the Tigers from 1952 to 1954, never lost to Kansas. In fact, Pete said that he's the only Ekern to never lose to the Jayhawks *and* to Mexico High School's archrival Fulton High School.

In Missouri's 10–6 victory over Kansas in Lawrence in 1953, a massive bench-clearing brawl marked the end of the game. The brawl ensued after one of Missouri's players stripped the ball, forcing a fumble late in the game.

"Games were always tougher against Kansas," Pete said. "As my kids grew up, I remember telling them the week before the Kansas game each year to get ready. It was almost time to burn Lawrence again."

During his playing days, Pete worked in the equipment room washing uniforms, socks, and jocks and repairing and cleaning helmets. He earned about fifteen dollars a month. After earning his bachelor's degree Pete attended the University of Missouri medical school, and during his first or second year of graduate work, he watered Faurot Field in the evenings, making sure the sprinklers didn't get hung up. The fifteen a month he earned for that was enough to pay his bills.

Pete later returned to Mexico, where he opened a medical practice. Sons Andy and Kirk both excelled at the same high school as their dad but had to walk on at Missouri before earning scholarships.

"There was no way I wasn't going to go to Mizzou," Andy said. "I grew up hearing all the stories of my dad and uncle . . . how Bert made All–Big Six . . . how my granddad took the train to New Orleans to watch Bert play in the Sugar Bowl against Fordham . . . how much we don't like Kansas.

"I wasn't going anywhere but Mizzou. I was a walk-on, but Mizzou had a great walk-on program. All I was asking for was a chance to play. The coach told us that if we worked hard, we would be given every chance to make the team."

As a kid, Andy listened on the radio to Missouri's thrilling upsets over Alabama (1975), Ohio State (1976), and Nebraska (1978). One of the greatest moments of his Mizzou career was the Tigers' upset over Oklahoma 19–14 at home in 1981. It was Missouri's first victory over the Sooners in eleven seasons.

During his junior season, Andy had a Kansas experience similar to his dad's. The Jayhawks won the game, and Kansas fans stormed the field, causing another brawl. One of Andy's best friends on the Tigers team walked away with a Jayhawks helmet.

Sally Ruth Ekern, sister to Bert, Bill, Pete, George, and Carol, was an excellent athlete in her own right. She could throw a football so much better than the boys in junior high school that the Mexico locals whisked her mother out of town for a day so Sally Ruth could play for the boys' junior high team. Her exploits made local and national news. Sally Ruth eventually got her doc-

The University of Missouri adopted the nickname Tigers to honor the citizens of Columbia, who banded together during the Civil War to protect the town.

torate at the University of Wisconsin—the proper way to throw a football was part of her thesis.

The only Ekern to resist Mizzou was Carl, Bill's youngest son. When Bill moved his family to California, Carl decided to attend San Jose State University. From there, he went on to an impressive NFL career with the Los Angeles Rams.

Pete Ekern still has his father's seats at Memorial Stadium. He'll continue to keep them warm as the next generation of Ekerns prepares to fight for Ol' Mizzou.

Show Me Some Football

Some of the most famous writers in American history—among them Mark Twain, Tennessee Williams, T. S. Eliot, and Laura Ingalls Wilder—have called Missouri home for a time during their lives. These Show-Me State authors and playwrights created some of literature's most memorable fictional characters.

Reality has a way of developing its own legendary figures, too, and the early years of football at the University of Missouri produced an assortment of amazing tales. In fact, Missouri football did a better job of attracting unique characters to the gridiron than it did capturing championships from 1890 to 1934.

College football in the late 1800s and early 1900s was not the glamorous and extravagant show that is watched by millions today. Missouri football began humbly, in 1890, when a group of students ordered a ball in the mail. When it arrived, the students were shocked by its shape and had little idea exactly how to play the game.

More than three decades later, before the 1922 Homecoming game against Kansas, Burton Thompson, a fullback on Mizzou's inaugural team, recalled the difficulty of getting twenty-two young men to participate in the initial tryouts. "Many of the student body [which numbered 600 at the time] preferred to stand on the sidelines and hurl derisive comments at our efforts, which they considered a huge comedy," he said.

In those early days college teams got three downs to go five yards for a first down. A field goal was worth 5 points, a touchdown 4, and the conversion after a touchdown 2. Most fields consisted mainly of dirt (which turned to thick clay mud over the course of a game), rocks, and weeds and were marked at different lengths. In 1896 a Missouri player by the last name of Tucker had a 115-yard touchdown run against Nebraska. Rollins Field, where the Tigers played, was 116 yards long. There were rumblings that Tucker may have been a professional and therefore ineligible.

Princeton, Rutgers, Harvard, Yale, and a few other East Coast institutions were the pioneers of American football in that era. The migration of players from those universities helped bring the game west. Mizzou's first coach was Austin L. McRae, a physics professor from Harvard. The Black and Gold team (MU had not yet adopted the Tiger as its mascot) defeated a team of lawyers and another loosely organized team from within the school as tune-ups for the big game with Washington University in St. Louis. Mizzou was soundly defeated 23–0 by the Bears; thus the school finished 2–1 in its inaugural campaign.

McRae lasted one season and was followed by Hal Reid (1891), E. H. Jones from Colgate (1892), and H. L. Robinson (1893–94), who had starred at Tufts College in Boston. Robinson did not earn a salary because he also was enrolled in Missouri as an engineering student. C. D. "Pop" Bliss (1895) and Frank Patterson (1896) both hailed from Yale and coached Missouri until Charles Young, in 1897, became the first Missouri alumnus to be named coach of the team. Two Brown University teammates, David L. Fultz (1898–99) and Fred Murphy (1900–1901), ushered Missouri football into the twentieth century.

College football scheduling was erratic — to say the least — before the turn of the century. A list of opponents and a season schedule could be summed up mainly as "anyone, anytime, and almost anyplace." Even so, it seems that the 1896 Missouri Tigers football team took this philosophy a little too seriously.

Mizzou finished its regular season 3–5 (including a demoralizing 30–0 loss to Kansas) and promptly scheduled a December game against the Dallas Athletic Club in Texas. After punishing the Dallas team 28–0, the Tigers were persuaded by two Texas businessmen to go on a barnstorming trip through Texas and into Mexico.

There was one problem with agreeing to travel out of the country: School was in session, and the Tigers' players did not

The inaugural Missouri football team, shown here in 1890, ordered their first football through the mail.

have notes excusing them from class. Missouri did not surrender a point to three opponents, defeating Texas 10–0, the Austin Mules 39–0, and a team from San Antonio 29–0. Missouri won a fourth game, 21–10, over an Austin YMCA team. Between Christmas and New Year's Day, Missouri played a couple of exhibition games in Mexico City. The Tigers traveled by train and arrived back in Columbia on January 4, 1897. University officials were understandably upset at the twenty-five-day, 6,000-mile excursion.

"While their [the Tigers' players] conduct was not at all times strictly decorous, they were always gentlemen and were ever mindful of the duty they owed the school and their state," wrote a reporter for Missouri's yearbook, *The Savitar*.

In 1902 Pat O'Dea became Mizzou's coach. Because American football partly finds its roots in rugby, it isn't that surprising that 6-foot, 170-pound O'Dea, who emigrated from Australia to the United States to attend the University of Wisconsin, was one of the sport's earliest legends. What is surprising is that he landed in Columbia to coach the Tigers.

O'Dea went to Wisconsin because his brother was coaching track and field there. During his career with the Badgers, Pat O'Dea earned the nickname the Kangaroo Kicker by dropkicking a 62-yard field goal and sending a punt 87 yards against Northwestern in 1898. He reportedly had a 110-yard punt against Minnesota and a 100-yard effort against Yale. O'Dea also was a sprinter who returned a kickoff 90 yards for a touchdown against Beloit College. (He added four field goals in that game.)

No one can say for sure whether O'Dea's disappointing 5–3 season at Missouri is what caused him to give up football and move to California, but regardless, O'Dea eventually dropped completely out of the public eye. There were rumors he was killed while serving in the Australian Army in World War I.

However, Bill Leiser, sports editor of the *San Francisco Chronicle*, discovered in 1934 that O'Dea had changed his name to Charles Mitchell and was working as an accountant for a lumber company in Westwood, California. Apparently, O'Dea had just become tired of being a football celebrity. Born on St. Patrick's Day in 1872, O'Dea died one day after being elected into the College Football Hall of Fame in 1962.

Clark W. Hetherington was hired as Missouri's first athletic director the year following the football team's escapade in Mexico, and the Stanford professor brought discipline and organization to the Tigers' athletic programs from 1897 to 1908. However, Hetherington was a cold individual who eventually alienated himself from students, staff, and, most important, alumni.

John McLean (1903–05) followed O'Dea as the Tigers' head football coach and posted a 9–17–1 record. McLean was succeeded by W. J. Monilaw, who won eighteen games in three seasons before giving way to William Roper in 1909. Roper led the Tigers to an undefeated season in 1909 but was replaced by William Hollenbeck in 1910.

In 1911 Chester Brewer, who had been a star athlete at the University of Wisconsin and the first athletic director at Michigan State University, was brought to Columbia to replace Hetherington as athletic director and to coach the football team. After a dismal first season (2–4–2), Brewer captured a Missouri Valley Conference championship in 1913.

Although the warm-hearted Brewer was successful as a football coach, his real talents lay in being both athletic director and cheerleader. He had an uncanny creative flair for increasing enthusiasm and support among Mizzou fans.

In 1911, in the first-ever Homecoming game, Brewer called upon Missouri fans to come back home to Columbia for the Tigers' game against Kansas. More than 9,000 Mizzou faithful overflowed Rollins Field and witnessed a 3–3 tie. That weekend Brewer paid special tribute to the 1890 Tigers team and presented official letters to every person who played in the pre-letterman era.

Brewer directed the building of the first concrete stands at Rollins Field (1911), Memorial Stadium (1926), and Brewer Field House (1930). He spent most of the final forty-two years of his life on the Columbia campus.

Brewer coached the Tigers until 1914, when he gave way to H. F. Schulte. Brewer remained as the school's athletic director until 1918. In four seasons, Schulte led Mizzou to sixteen victories.

One of Schulte's key players was Anton Stankowski, who became a fixture in Missouri football, from his freshman season as a player in 1914 until his death at the age of eighty-four in 1979. The diminutive 5-foot 6-inch, 132-pound Stankowski stood tall as a Tigers quarterback, coach, administrator, and historian.

The Greatest Tiger Team Ever

Missouri Tigers football never tasted an official championship during its first nineteen seasons. But that changed in 1909, when MU professor W. G. Manly took a trip to the East Coast and came back with twenty-nine-year-old Princeton graduate William B. Roper as coach.

"Roper felt that football was 90 percent fight and all the rest was 10 percent," said Charley Caldwell, who succeeded Roper at Princeton, in *Ol' Mizzou: A Century of Tiger Football.* "He was a great psychologist. He would use anything to take advantage. He was wonderful in talking to the team. He was more than just a coach. He was a great man."

Roper did more than just defeat Kansas in 1909. He guided the Tigers to the Missouri Valley Conference title and the only undefeated season (7–0–1) in school history. The victory over Kansas was especially sweet, as both teams had entered the Thanksgiving Day contest with zero losses.

Mizzou, however, had only one magical season with Roper. The Missouri alumni could not match Princeton's $5,000 salary offer. Roper returned to his alma mater and guided that school to an 89–28–16 record in twenty seasons—while also working as a lawyer, politician, and insurance salesman.

Stankowski was so adept at carrying out coach Schulte's game plan that everyone called him the General. During the 1916 season Stankowski played all but fifteen minutes of an eight-game schedule.

Stankowski's size, which was small even for his era, gave him a great advantage in the original T formation. He would take the snap from center by squatting so low that few defenders could see him. Once he took the snap, his speed and agility allowed him to get past defenders before they knew what happened.

In the 1970s Stankowski talked about his time at Missouri with legendary *St. Louis Post-Dispatch* sports editor and columnist Bob Broeg. "I believe we had more deception then," Stankowski told Broeg, "but now it's all power and speed. The second incomplete pass in a series of downs then brought a five-yard penalty."

One of the General's favorite memories was an incident during a 23–14 victory over Oklahoma in 1916. The Tigers had played poorly throughout the first half and trailed at the intermission. Teams did not have locker rooms at the time, so they stayed on the field during halftime. In an attempt to motivate his players, Coach Shulte told them to look at his wife, who was crying at the end of the Missouri bench.

"Coach said, 'Look at Chum [the nickname the players had given Shulte's wife],'" Stankowski told Broeg. "I guess you could say we won that game for Chum." Stankowski and Harry Viner were each awarded half the game ball for propelling the team to victory.

Stankowski played at Missouri from 1914 to 1919, a stint that was interrupted by service in World War I. He went on to coach

What's in a Name?

It seems that players in the early years of college football could not be considered authentic unless they had a nickname. Missouri's early lettermen had more than their share of interesting monikers. Here are just a few of them:

- James "Fats" Gallagher was a 215-pound tackle good enough to be chosen alongside more prominent Big Ten players on the All-Western Team in 1913.

- Joe "Puny" Bluck was a 220-pound (massive for that time) tackle in 1909.

- Graham Hall on the Missouri campus is named after Robert "Peaches" Graham, who played on the 1914 Tigers team and was killed in World War I.

- Ed "Brick" Travis was a two-way tackle and the first Missouri player inducted into the National College Football Foundation Hall of Fame.

Ed "Brick" Travis

- Huston "Hoot" Betty blocked a punt that led to the game-winning touchdown in a 24–21 victory over Oklahoma in 1936.

- All-America "Pitchin' Paul" Christman is considered the greatest quarterback in Missouri history. He led the Tigers to a Big Six Championship and to the 1940 Orange Bowl and the 1942 Sugar Bowl.

- Henry "Slippery" Ice ran for a school record 240 yards on just eight carries against archrival Kansas in 1941.

California Dreamin'

The Roaring Twenties were a time of tremendous change in the United States, and the end of the 1924 football season at the University of Missouri marked a movement to national prominence. After capturing the Missouri Valley Conference championship, the Tigers received an unexpected invitation to travel to Los Angeles and play a Christmas game against the University of Southern California Trojans.

The Trojans and the Stanford Cardinal were co-champions of the Pacific Coast Conference, but thanks to legendary running back Ernie Nevers's star power, the Cardinal received the invitation to play Notre Dame in the Rose Bowl in Pasadena, California. The city of Los Angeles searched the country for the next-best team. Mizzou had defeated Big Ten champion Chicago during the year and thus was selected to make the cross-country trip. It was great timing: The Tigers had begun raising money for a new stadium, and this trip would provide a great opportunity to generate much-needed funds.

On December 19 the Missouri entourage left Columbia by train in a driving sleet storm. The journey included dinners and events hosted by Missouri alumni in various states. On December 23 the Tigers arrived in Los Angeles and were greeted by the mayor and the USC band, which escorted the players to the Ambassador Hotel.

The parties and sightseeing didn't slow down when the Tigers got to L.A. The team made trips to San Pedro, Catalina Island, and San Francisco; toured the USS Maryland; and visited Metro-Goldwyn-Mayer studios, where they met Rudolf Valentino, William S. Hart, Blanche Sweet, and Lon Chaney. Kansas City native Chuck Lewis, who starred as a runner, passer, and dropkicker for the Tigers from 1919 to 1921, had moved to Hollywood after college and become a personal trainer for Douglas Fairbanks, Jr. Lewis arranged a private studio party for the Tigers.

Sandwiched between all the extracurricular activities, the game against USC was anticlimactic. Missouri lost 20–7 before 40,000 fans at the Los Angeles Memorial Coliseum. (The crowd also served as scenery for a silent motion-picture comedy, *The Freshman*, that was filmed during the game.) Despite the loss, the trip was a huge financial success for Mizzou, which had a net profit of $50,000 on the season.

high school sports in St. Joseph, Missouri, until 1926, when he returned to Mizzou's campus in Columbia. After serving as an assistant football coach until 1934, Stankowski became the driving force for the university's intramural program.

Chester Brewer left the athletic director post at Missouri at the end of World War I and returned to Michigan State. Without Brewer at the helm, the Tigers experienced success on the field, but too much discord off it. Brewer returned as athletic director in 1923 and stayed another thirty years until his death at age seventy-seven.

Shortly after Brewer resumed his duties, and just three weeks before the 1923 season, he hired a thin Texan named Gwinn Henry to coach the football team. Henry's easygoing demeanor contrasted sharply with his predecessors and helped him connect with his players and the fans.

On the field, things did not start as rosy for Henry. The team finished a disappointing 2–3–3, but there were a couple of watershed games that season. After years of mounting losses to Nebraska and Kansas, the new coach was able to post ties against each of them, which was enough for Missouri fans. During his nine-year run as the Tigers' head coach, Henry was able to defeat or tie Nebraska and Kansas a total of ten times.

"[Henry] was a great person and the greatest handling a squad," Emmett R. (Abe) Stuber, who played for Henry and later became a college football coach, told Broeg. "He had the ability to get players to play and to make the big plays. They said Henry was only so-so as an offensive coach, but the fact is that he was a very good pass coach, using his backs to slip out of the backfield with good patterns."

Don Faurot excelled in football, basketball, and baseball during his undergraduate days at Mizzou.

Despite the poor 1923 record, Henry had a very talented group of players, and it didn't take them long to gel into a champion team. Led by players such as Art Bond (a Rhodes Scholar and father of U.S. Senator Christopher "Kit" Bond), center Clyde Smith, tackles Ed Lindenmeyer and Charles (Chase) Van Dyne, guard Jerry Lewis, and backs Stuber and an agricultural student named Don Faurot, Mizzou opened the 1924 season with an amazing 3–0 upset over the University of Chicago, coached by the legendary Amos Alonzo Stagg.

The Tigers finished the regular season with a 7–1 record and captured the first of their three Missouri Valley Championships over the next four years. From 1924 to 1927 Henry led the team to twenty-five victories, including a 9–6 defeat of Nebraska in 1925, the first time the Tigers had defeated the Cornhuskers since 1899.

"Except for Dan Devine's 1969 team, I don't believe any of our teams ever rated higher than Henry's," Faurot told Broeg in *Ol' Mizzou: A Century of Tiger Football*. "There were no coaches or press polls in Henry's day."

It was a memorable time for Mizzou football. Running back Bert Clark was a scoring machine in three games against Nebraska. He caught a touchdown pass in the 1925 victory, returned a punt for a touchdown, had a scoring reception in a 14–7 win in 1926, and had another touchdown reception in a 7–6 victory in 1927. Lindenmeyer became Missouri's first All-American. The Tigers' fortunes were up, and the 25,000-seat Memorial Stadium replaced Rollins Field in 1926.

Probably Henry's greatest legacy at Mizzou was his tutelage of Faurot. Not only would Faurot become the most influential force in Missouri football history, but he would also earn national acclaim as one of the sport's greatest innovators.

Mr. Missouri Football

Just outside Mizzou's Memorial Stadium stands a nine-foot bronzed statue of legendary Tiger player, coach, and administrator Don Faurot. As massive as the statue is, it doesn't come close to casting over Missouri's football program the enveloping shadow that Faurot himself produced during the past seven decades. The college football landscape is littered with awe-inspiring, irrepressible figures whose names are synonymous with their institutions. When you think of Alabama, Paul "Bear" Bryant immediately comes to mind. At Penn State it's Joe Paterno. Bobby Bowden is Florida State. And Eddie Robinson ruled at Grambling. Missouri has Don Faurot.

"He was the University of Missouri," said Warren Powers, who coached the Tigers from 1978 to 1984. "As long as the university was around, Don Faurot was around."

In fact, Faurot is as much the core of Missouri football as John Wooden is UCLA basketball. Faurot's imprint also extends beyond the city limits of Columbia, Missouri, to the explosion of the game of football across the country.

"He had more to do with the history of football and athletics in general at the University of Missouri than any other man, and he'll be sorely missed," then Tigers head football coach Larry Smith said after Faurot died at ninety-three on October 19, 1995.

"If everybody in collegiate athletics was a Don Faurot, then collegiate athletics would be what it is supposed to be," former Big Eight and Big Ten commissioner Wayne Duke once said.

Faurot didn't grow up in an era when fathers dreamed of their children becoming the next child sports prodigy, performing in front of thousands of fans and earning millions of dollars. In fact, during Faurot's youth real men were judged by the size of their herds and expanse of their farmland, not by the number of touchdowns they scored.

Faurot was born in Mountain Grove, Missouri. His father moved the family around the state in search of the best farming experience. When Don, the oldest of four boys, decided to attend the University of Missouri, it was to learn how to start an orchard business, not to build championship sports teams. For the agri-

Don Faurot was one of the most innovative football coaches in NCAA history. He also knew how to beat Kansas.

culture major, sports were just an enjoyable diversion from what really mattered in life.

Don't think that Faurot didn't love playing sports, however. As a youth living in Columbia, he used to sneak into Rollins Field to watch the Tigers play football. Faurot excelled as an athlete and eventually played basketball, baseball, and football for Mizzou.

Initially Faurot earned a more prominent reputation as a captain on the basketball team and on the baseball team. His football prowess was limited by a boyhood farm accident that had cost him the top half of the first two fingers on his right hand. But from 1923 to 1924 he was a 145-pound linebacker and punter for the Tigers' football team.

The Tigers struggled to a 2–3–3 record in Faurot's first season. One of those losses came against Iowa State, and Faurot played a big part in the Cyclones' 2–0 victory. In a constant rain, Faurot punted the ball twenty times. As Faurot lined up near his own goal line for one punt, center Clyde Smith snapped the ball low through Faurot's hands, and it went through the end zone, giving Iowa State a safety and the game-winning points. Two weeks later, against Kansas State in similar weather conditions, the coaches asked Faurot to intentionally take a safety, but he refused. Mizzou's Art Bond took the safety instead of Faurot, and the Tigers won 4–2.

Faurot got his first taste of championship-level football as a senior. The Tigers defeated Amos Alonzo Stagg's Big Ten champion University of Chicago in the season's first game. Missouri went on to win seven of eight games, including a regular-season-ending 15–0 victory over Kansas.

It was during the losing campaign of 1923 that Faurot learned a valuable lesson, however.

With three games remaining in the season, Missouri lost a hard-fought contest with Oklahoma, 13–0. The final two opponents on the Tigers' schedule were Washington University and Kansas. Washington University had lost earlier in the year 62–7 to Oklahoma and 83–0 to Kansas. Knowing how important the Kansas game was to the Mizzou faithful and feeling that Washington University would not provide a stiff challenge, Tigers head coach Gwinn Henry decided to leave his team during the week before the game to scout the dreaded Jayhawks. The result was an embarrassing 13–7 loss to Washington. The Tigers rebounded for a 3–3 tie against Kansas, but Henry's actions made a big impression on one of his players. "I learned never to underestimate an opponent, [and] never to leave my team to scout a future foe," said Don Faurot in Bob Broeg's *Ol' Mizzou: A Century of Tiger Football*.

In 1935 Faurot, who had amassed a 63–13–3 record, including twenty-six consecutive victories, in nine seasons at Kirksville Teachers College (now named Truman State University after the former president), was introduced as head football coach at the University of Missouri. He replaced Frank Carideo, who had won only two games in three seasons.

In nineteen years as the Tigers' head coach, Faurot never took an opponent lightly and posted an impressive 101–79–10 record. He earned his first victory over Kansas in 1936 and helped turn the tide in the rivalry with a 13–4–2 overall record against the Jayhawks. From 1938 to 1943 Faurot guided Mizzou to twenty-two consecutive home victories and three Big Six Championships. Although he never won a bowl game, he took the Tigers to the postseason four times.

"He was a very, very tough coach on the field," said John Kadlec, a Missouri player, assistant coach, administrator, and broadcaster since 1946. "He was fair, but tough. He knew what it took to play football, and that meant discipline. I'll tell you this about Coach Faurot: I've never known another coach in the country who knew as much about the game. He could coach offense or defense. Some coaches major in one side or the other, but this guy was so adept that he could coach every position. He knew the guard, the tackle, and the end.

"Bob Broeg of the *St. Louis Post-Dispatch* said this, and I agree: 'He could take his eleven and beat you, then take your eleven and beat his.' He was a real student of the game. He coached defensive backs in the Blue-Gray game until he was about eighty-five years old. The head coaches down there were amazed at how contemporary he was on pass defense. He was a brilliant guy. He would go out and watch practice every day at Missouri in his later years."

The 1935 Tigers marked the beginning of Don Faurot's legendary coaching career at Mizzou.

Integrity and character were two hallmarks of Faurot's legacy as a coach. He had learned how to be a model citizen from his father F. W. (Fred) Faurot. Don actually earned a gold watch from F. W. by honoring his promise to his father to never drink or smoke. While Faurot was coaching at Mizzou, one of his players went 17 cents over his yearly allowable income, and the honest coach reported it to the NCAA.

Former Tiger Gus Entsminger, who played for Faurot and is considered one of college football's first great Split T formation quarterbacks, was involved in another example of Faurot's ideals. Entsminger, then a sophomore reserve, sat on the bench late in a rout against Iowa State, hoping to get into the game. When Entsminger finally got the call to go in, it was only to tell another player to allow the Cyclones to return an upcoming kickoff for a touchdown.

"I learned after the game this was not the first time that Don

The Scribe

Knute Rockne and Notre Dame had Grantland Rice. Don Faurot and the University of Missouri had Bob Broeg. Broeg has forgotten more about Mizzou football history than most books have retold. He has been the "unofficial" keeper of the flame when it comes to Tigers lore.

The St. Louis native graduated from the University of Missouri in 1941 with a bachelor's degree in journalism. More than three decades later, Broeg wrote the most definitive and exhaustive history of Missouri football—*Ol' Mizzou: A Story of Missouri Football*. In 1990 he revised and renamed the book *Ol' Mizzou: A Century of Tiger Football*.

Following stints with the Associated Press, *St. Louis Star Times*, and the U.S. Marines, Broeg began covering the Tigers and other sports for the *St. Louis Post-Dispatch* in 1947. He served variously as a writer, columnist, or sports editor for the *Post-Dispatch* for almost fifty years, retiring in 1985. During his illustrious career Broeg won numerous sportswriting awards, was president of the Baseball Writers Association of America, and voted for members of the college and pro football halls of fame.

Faurot extended the courtesy," Entsminger recalled in *Ol' Mizzou*. "He didn't want to embarrass the other team."

A significant philosophy of Faurot's was his policy to stay strictly within state lines when recruiting players. When members of the Jacksonville Navy team wanted to play for Faurot after World War II in 1946, he turned them down.

"If you win with players from afar, that's fine," Faurot told Broeg. "If you win with local boys, that's great. If you lose with your area kids, that's bad. If you go a distance to get them, alienating your own area high school coaches and fans, and then lose—that's terrible."

Faurot also believed in allowing large numbers of young men to try out for the team. In his first season at Missouri, he kept 118 players, a dramatic increase from previous seasons. "I don't believe in cutting anybody off the squad," he said to *St. Louis Post-Dispatch* writer James M. Gould in 1935. "It hurts the confidence of the boys. We're not dealing with ready-made varsity teams here. We've got to develop them from men who voluntarily chose the University as their school. We believe this developing is in the true spirit of college athletics. Besides, I didn't even make the Missouri team myself until what amounted to my fourth year!"

A member of the National Football Foundation, Missouri Sports, Orange Bowl, and Blue-Gray Game Halls of Fame, Faurot coached up to the time of his death. He helped select talent and coached for the Blue-Gray All-Star Game until 1994.

Faurot's Split T formation is his legacy to football strategy. Notre Dame's Knute Rockne is credited with creating football's forward pass. Amos Alonzo Stagg gave us the direct snap from center and the T formation. Cowboys head coach Tom Landry and 49ers head coach Bill Walsh, both members of the Pro Football Hall of Fame, designed the "Umbrella" defense and West Coast offense, respectively. Faurot belongs on this list of football luminaries who dramatically changed the game with their innovations. His Split T opened up the running game and dominated the college landscape after its inception in 1941.

"He [Faurot] made the only significant change in offensive football in, I used to say fifty years but now I'd say seventy-five years," Dan Devine said in 1995. "Almost everything is an off-shoot of his old Split T."

The genesis of the Split T, which essentially widened the spacing among the offensive linemen and provided more lanes to run through, was one part necessity and another part inspiration. When the Tigers lost to graduation pass-happy Paul Christman, whose arm they rode to win twenty games from 1938 to 1940 and earn a Big Six championship and Orange Bowl bid in 1939, Faurot needed to keep the momentum going. As the team entered the 1941 season, its strength lay at running back with Bob Steuber, Harry "Slippery" Ice, and Maurice "Red" Wade, and in the offensive line with All-America center Darold Jenkins, All–Big Six guard Mike Fitzgerald, and tackle Bob Jeffries.

Faurot's inspiration came from his days as captain of the MU basketball team. Faurot marveled at how a defender had to make a decision on two-on-one fast breaks. He wondered if you could force a defender to make a split-second choice in football.

With wider splits along the line, the quarterback could take the snap and hand off to a back diving straight into a hole or keep the ball and run down the line with his other running back close behind. On the keeper, when the quarterback reached the defensive end, he had the option to keep and run inside the defensive end or pitch it wide to his trailing running back. Offenses such as the Wishbone, Wingbone, Veer, and I formation are derivatives of Faurot's option play in the Split T.

The results of the new formation were devastating to Mizzou opponents. The Tigers had the top-ranked rushing offense in the

An Original Missouri Refrigerator

Long before Chicago Bears defensive tackle William "Refrigerator" Perry gained national fame for his mammoth frame and by scoring touchdowns as a part-time fullback, Missouri's Jim Kekeris was blasting open holes as an offensive tackle, rumbling for yardage as a fullback, and lighting up the college football world with his larger-than-life personality.

In 1944 Don Faurot was off serving in the U.S. military and Chauncey Simpson was struggling to win football games at Mizzou with a war-depleted roster. In the season-ending contest against Kansas, Simpson and assistant Herb Bunker decided to use the 270-pound tackle as a full-back in short-yardage and goal-line situations. Kekeris pounded the Jay-hawks' defensive line and had one run for 32 yards in the Tigers' 28–0 victory.

Kekeris, who had ballooned to 295 pounds, and diminutive quarter-back Leonard Brown, weighing in at just under 140 pounds, were the stars of Missouri's amazing 1945 campaign. Consisting mostly of kids too young for military service and wounded veterans, the Tigers opened with a 10–7 upset victory over Ohio State, thanks to Kekeris's blocking at tackle and his game-winning field goal. The following week Kekeris and Mizzou used a fake field goal attempt to set up a touchdown and a 14–6 victory over defending Big Six champion Oklahoma.

Missouri defeated Kansas 33–12 and captured the Big Six title with a 6–3 record. Kekeris was named to the All–Big Six team, earned second-team All-America honors, and was later chosen for the all-time Cotton Bowl team for his play in Missouri's 40–27 loss to Texas and its quarter-back (and future Pro Football Hall of Famer) Bobby Layne.

Kekeris eventually took his size and act to the NFL, playing for the Philadelphia Eagles in 1947 and the Green Bay Packers in 1948.

nation in 1941, averaging nearly 308 yards per game and more than 5.6 yards per carry. Steuber (855 rushing yards), Wade (681), and Ice (603) were the top three runners in the conference.

Missouri won the 1941 Big Six Championship with an 8–1 record. The Tigers scored 226 points and held opponents to just 39. The only thing to slow down the Spilt T was the rain sitting on the slippery turf of Tulane Stadium in the 1942 Sugar Bowl. Unable to gain traction, Mizzou fell to Fordham, 2–0.

"We never had to hold our blocks as long as we did in the Single Wing offense," Jenkins told Missouri sports information director Bill Callahan years later. "Also, playing defense against the Single Wing, linebackers had to wait a full count before committing themselves. If they waited a full count against the Split T, all they saw were cleats."

The only mistake Faurot made in creating the Split T was sharing it with others. Playing in an era well before computerized scouting of opponents or even video tape, the only way to pass along strategic secrets was to share them with assistants.

After winning a second consecutive Big Six title with the Split T in 1942, Faurot left Columbia to serve in the military as a coach at Iowa Pre-Flight and Jacksonville. Two of Faurot's assistants, Jim Tatum and Bud Wilkinson, went on to use versions of the option in the Split T (Tatum at the University of Maryland and Wilkinson at Oklahoma) to eventually terrorize Missouri and the rest of college football.

Though college football eventually caught up to his Split T, Faurot never stopped innovating. Not even a meeting with the president of the United States kept Faurot from working on his game plans. In 1948 Faurot was scheduled to meet with President Truman after the team's game against Navy in Baltimore. However, he lost track of time while talking with Tatum and drawing up new plays on a napkin while sitting in a Maryland restaurant, and he almost missed his date with the president.

When Faurot became Missouri's head coach and athletic director, not only did he inherit a losing club on the field, but he also inherited an athletic program that was nearly a half-million dollars in debt and foundering. As Missouri's athletic director, from 1935 to 1967, Faurot made significant strides in turning the university into a national sports power.

Football generated the lion's share of the university's athletics budget. One of Faurot's first changes was to schedule tougher opponents on the road to begin each season, which would in turn generate bigger paydays. For example, between 1939 and 1949 the Tigers faced the Ohio State Buckeyes nine times, playing them in either the first or second game of each season. Only once did the Buckeyes travel to Columbia, and the Tigers could muster only one tie and eight losses. Missouri also played Michigan in Ann Arbor, Wisconsin in Madison, Texas in Austin, and SMU (six times) in Dallas.

"Missouri owes a debt to Ohio State," said former Mizzou athletic administrator Sam Shirky in *Ol' Mizzou*, "and to Don Faurot. To Ohio State for giving us the opening-game series and to Faurot for his willingness to play it. That series, more than any other, permitted Don to wipe out athletic-department indebtedness."

In 1942 Faurot scheduled three extra games against tough military teams to earn the team more money. His business acumen even extended to the selection of bowl games. Following the 1941 season, the Rose Bowl hinted at offering the Tigers a bid, but when the Bowl hesitated with the invitation, Faurot—against the wishes of others at Mizzou—decided to accept a bid to the Sugar Bowl.

With wartime gas rationing, the closer game allowed more Tigers fans to attend. The Sugar Bowl payday of $75,000 was $2,000 more than Missouri's entire athletic department budget when Faurot took over in 1935.

Faurot had an eye for coaching talent. His coaching tree included Phil Bengtson, who went on to replace Vince Lombardi as head coach of the Green Bay Packers; Dan Devine, the winningest coach in Mizzou history, who later won a national title with the Notre Dame Fighting Irish and replaced Bengtson as the Packers' head coach; Bud Wilkinson, who took the Split T formation to even greater success, winning three national championships and an NCAA-record forty-seven consecutive games at Oklahoma; Jim Tatum, who later won a national title at Maryland; and Frank Broyles, who would win 144 games, seven Southwest Conference titles, and the 1964 national championship at Arkansas.

Faurot also made impressive coaching hires off the football field. John "Hi" Simmons led the Tigers to eleven Big Six Championships in baseball, and Tom Botts coached the Missouri track team for twenty-six years, winning a cross-country national title and two Big Eight Championships. Botts was the NCAA Coach of the Year in 1970. Between 1935 and the start of World War II, the Tigers won at least one Big Six title each year in either football, baseball, basketball, or track.

"Don is a wonderful man," said Devine following Faurot's death. "I love that guy. He was the best athletic director I ever worked under, and I've worked under some good ones."

All-American Boys

Al Onofrio, who served as head football coach for the University of Missouri from 1971 to 1977, once offered one of the most accurate assessments of the players who have graced the turf of Faurot Field. "I'm sold on Missouri as a state and as a university, and as a people," said Onofrio after deciding to take over for departing legend Dan Devine rather than accompany Devine to his next stop with the NFL's Green

Bay Packers. "I've learned over the years here, recruiting with and for Dan, that we're blessed with a tough, dedicated kind of kid who is a credit to himself and his family. It's the kind who too often might be built for strength, rather than speed, and we've been fortunate to implement our recruiting with an occasional great player from elsewhere. But, year in and year out, we've won with what we basically get from this area. It's talent without temperament."

Quarterback "Pitchin' Paul" Christman, running back/defensive back Johnny Roland, cornerback Roger Wehrli, and tight end Kellen Winslow generally have been considered the greatest of the players about whom Onofrio spoke so eloquently and lovingly. Those four may also be the most emblematic of the type of player he described. In the current era, defensive end Justin Smith, who is still cementing his legacy in the NFL, should be added to that list.

Each of these players possessed different athletic abilities that brought the Tigers success. However, they also had a lot in common. With their grit, determination, desire, and humility they all set the standard of what it takes to be a letterman for Ol' Mizzou.

Center Stage: All-America Quarterback Paul Christman

From the first football snap at Missouri until 1937, the Tigers were a good, rough-and-tumble team, but they lacked any distinguishing characteristics that could place them on the national stage with programs such as Michigan, the University of Chicago, Notre Dame, Stanford, or Southern California. In 1937 Kansas City Associated Press sports editor Skipper Patrick told MU ath-

Paul Christman was nicknamed "Pitchin' Paul" for his passing prowess.

letic advisor Sam Shirky that the Tigers needed a box-office player to complete coach Don Faurot's turnaround of Mizzou football. Patrick also pointed out to Shirky that the player he needed— quarterback Paul Christman—was currently on Missouri's freshman team.

Christman wasn't a great runner, but the 6-foot, 195-pound son of a printer for the *St. Louis Post-Dispatch* had movie star looks, above-average intelligence, and a slingshot for a right arm. Patrick turned out to be a prophet. From 1938 to 1940 "Pitchin' Paul"—as Patrick nicknamed him—guided the Tigers to twenty victories in twenty-eight games and helped Missouri become a national power.

It didn't take Christman long to prove he was exceptional. In a scrimmage before the 1938 season, he threw six touchdown passes in a 103–6 victory over the freshman squad. The rest of that year, which included key victories over Nebraska and Kansas, proved to be a harbinger of things to come for Christman and the Tigers.

"I've often thought how Faurot was considered conservative and a disciplinarian, but proving that he was indeed a good leader, he gave Paul considerable leeway, and we all profited from it," said end Bud Orf, a childhood friend and Tigers teammate of Christman.

In 1939 Christman led Mizzou to an 8–1 record, the first Big Six championship for Faurot, and an opportunity to play Georgia Tech in the Orange Bowl. Throughout the season, Christman, who finished third behind Iowa's Nile Kinnick and Michigan's Tom Harmon in Heisman Trophy voting, provided one highlight after another.

Before a 27–13 victory over Nebraska, Christman boasted to Associated Press writer Bob Broeg that he would "pass the bums of the stadium by half." Christman had three touchdown passes before halftime.

Against New York University at Yankee Stadium, Christman wowed national writers such as Grantland Rice by running for 54 yards and passing for 203. The 20–7 victory, which included two Christman touchdown runs and a touchdown pass, cemented All-America status for the signal caller.

Missouri's All-America center Darold Jenkins said the quarterback could "throw a football into a pickle barrel from 70 yards away." Christman made All-America and finished fifth in the Heisman balloting in 1941, but the Tigers just missed another

The All-Americans

Since 1988 the landscaping around the University of Missouri's athletic facilities has dramatically improved. What does this have to do with the university's football team? At least twenty-six trees around the stadium, Brookfield/Taylor Training Facility, and other prominent facilities were planted as part of the All-American Tree Project to honor the twenty-six first-team All-Americans who have played for the Tigers. Tackle Ed Lindenmeyer became Mizzou's first All-American in 1925, and six Tiger players—center Darold Jenkins (1941), end Danny LaRose (1960), defensive backs Johnny Roland (1965) and Roger Wehrli (1968), tight end Kellen Winslow (1978), and tackle John Clay (1986)—were unanimous selections.

Big Six title, losing to Nebraska and Oklahoma.

A member of the College Football Hall of Fame and chosen as the number-one player on Mizzou's All-Century Team in 1990, Christman is one of only nine Missouri passers to throw for more than 300 yards in a game (311 versus Kansas State in 1938). He was the first passer in Tigers history to accomplish the feat, and Mizzou didn't have another 300-yard passer until Tony Scardino threw for 365 against Oklahoma in 1951.

Christman led the Tigers in scoring and touchdowns in 1938 and 1939. His career passing records at Missouri stood for thirty years.

The youngest of seven children, Christman initially wanted to follow his brother Mark, a third baseman for the Detroit Tigers and St. Louis Browns, into professional baseball. And he almost never graced Faurot Field with his presence because he originally attended Purdue. However, Christman was ignored and homesick at Purdue, so he headed for mid-Missouri to join his other Maplewood (Missouri) High School teammates on the Tigers' squad.

Christman was a second-round draft choice of the Chicago Cardinals in 1941, but he didn't play his first game for the team until 1945 because he served in the Navy during World War II. As a rookie, Christman led the NFL with 219 passing attempts.

In 1947 Christman passed for 2,191 yards and teamed with backs Charley Trippi, Elmer Angsman, and Pat Harder to form the Cardinals' "Million Dollar Backfield." The offensive exploits of the backfield carried Chicago to a 9–3 record, including an impressive 28–21 victory over Philadelphia in the NFL Championship Game.

Christman played two more seasons with the Cardinals and finished his NFL career with the Green Bay Packers in 1950. He was a renowned football broadcaster on national television before his untimely death from a heart attack at age fifty-one.

Triple Threat: All-America Defensive Back Johnny Roland

During the final thirteen years of Don Faurot's coaching career at Missouri, Oklahoma's Bud Wilkinson, who had once been an assistant to Faurot and had based his vaunted option offense on the Split T formation he learned from Faurot, was a thorn in the

Tigers' side. The Sooners and Wilkinson had a 13–0 record against Mizzou, including victories of 41–7 in 1948, 41–7 in '50, 47–7 in '52, 20–0 in '55, and 67–14 in '56.

With Dan Devine at the helm, Missouri finally defeated the Sooners and Wilkinson in 1960, and in 1962 the team got an extra measure of revenge off the field by winning the recruiting battle for gifted running back Johnny Roland from Roy Miller High School in Corpus Christi, Texas. Roland was one of Oklahoma's top recruits, and the Sooners actually signed the 6-foot 2-inch, 207-pound speedster to a letter of intent. However, at that time letters of intent did not lock players to universities as they do today. Roland felt that as an African American he would have a better opportunity for a job after college in either Kansas City or St. Louis, and he also knew that Devine had established a good rapport with African Americans. He backed out of his commitment and headed for Columbia, Missouri.

Roland proved an electric performer from his first game as a Tiger until his last. In the 1962 season opener against the University of California in Berkeley, he rushed for 171 yards on 20 carries and scored 3 touchdowns.

Later in the year, Roland ran for 155 yards against Oklahoma and 104 against Iowa State. Overall, he led the team and ranked seventh in the nation with 830 rushing yards (5.2 yards per carry) and was ninth in the nation in scoring with 78 points (13 touchdowns). Mizzou finished Roland's sophomore season ranked twelfth in the nation and defeated Georgia Tech 14–10 in the Bluebonnet Bowl.

Unfortunately, Roland was dismissed from the team in 1963 when his car was discovered with stolen tires on it. A teammate

All-American Johnny Roland was equally dangerous as a running back or a defensive back.

had pulled a prank on Roland by switching Roland's tires with those of a nearby car, but Roland refused to turn in his teammate. Roland spent the year working in Kansas City.

When Roland returned to Columbia, Devine decided to move his star running back to defensive back. As the Tigers' co-captain in 1965, Roland propelled the team to an 8–2–1 record, including a 20–18 victory over Steve Spurrier and Florida in the Sugar Bowl. Roland became the first African American at Missouri to earn All-America honors—and he did it as a defensive back.

Legendary *St. Louis Post-Dispatch* scribe Bob Broeg said that Roland was the best all-around player on offense and defense in Tigers football history. Roland also was a dangerous return man, leading the Tigers in punt-return average in 1964 and '65 and in kickoff-return average in 1962 and '64.

Fittingly, Roland's college career ended much as it had begun. In his final regular-season game, he helped the Tigers trounce Kansas 44–20 by intercepting a pass, recovering a fumble, and returning a punt for 35 yards. He also played offense, completing and catching a pass. Roland was involved in a total of 19 plays, gained 178 yards, and scored 3 touchdowns.

Roland was a first-round draft choice of both the NFL's St. Louis Cardinals and the AFL's New York Jets in 1966. Former Missouri football great Jim Kekeris was Roland's agent, and Kekeris persuaded him that St. Louis offered greater opportunities for a Mizzou grad than the Big Apple.

The Cardinals switched Roland back to running back, and he earned NFL Rookie of the Year honors by gaining 695 rushing yards and 213 receiving yards and running for 5 touchdowns. He also scored a touchdown on a punt return and threw a touchdown pass.

Roland's best season in his eight-year NFL career came in 1967. He ran for 876 yards and 10 touchdowns and had 269 receiving yards and 1 touchdown reception. Overall as a pro, Roland had 3,750 rushing yards, 28 rushing touchdowns, 1,430 receiving yards, 6 touchdown receptions, and 2 scores on punt returns.

Roland's playing career was cut short by a knee injury in 1973. With his playing days behind him, Roland bought a radio station in St. Louis and embarked on a long NFL coaching career as an assistant with the Packers, Eagles, Bears, Giants, Cardinals, and Rams. A member of the College Football Hall of Fame, he coached running backs such as Walter Payton, Jerome Bettis, and other NFL 1,000-yard rushers.

Despite his exploits, Mizzou and Devine didn't retire Roland's jersey. Instead Devine decided to give the number to a player with raw talent whom he wanted to motivate. That player was defensive back Roger Wehrli.

Diamond in the Rough: All-America Defensive Back Roger Wehrli

Even in the current era of intense college football recruiting, it's doubtful that any prominent university would know about—or take seriously—a football, basketball, and track star athlete who starred at a high school that had a graduating class of twenty-eight people. In the case of Roger Wehrli, you can chalk one up to divine intervention.

Wehrli hailed from King City, Missouri, population 1,000. Small universities were interested in him, but more for his basketball prowess than football.

"Being from such a small school, we weren't really scouted," Wehrli said. "In fact, as far as Missouri goes, I wasn't scouted at all in football. They did send the freshman basketball coach down our senior year to watch one of our basketball games, thinking they might be interested in me in basketball. But after I took my football pads off after my final high school game, I thought it would be the last time."

At the state track meet late in his senior year of high school, Wehrli won the high and low hurdles and the long jump (he also medaled in the 220-yard dash). His performance in that meet, coupled with the recommendation of a Tigers assistant football coach who just happened to see Wehrli on film, prompted head coach Dan Devine to offer the football team's final scholarship in 1965 to Wehrli.

When Wehrli finally arrived in Columbia, Tigers coaches knew they had an extremely talented athlete. However, they struggled to decide on which side of the ball he should play.

"Even going into my freshman year, I didn't know until after a couple weeks of practice that they had me as a defensive player instead of an offensive player," Wehrli said. "We all were going through the same drills during two-a-days. When we went into spring ball my freshman year, there were several of us working out at defensive back. They moved one to wide receiver and put me in at defensive back. I can't remember if I knew for sure I was in the starting lineup in spring ball, because you kind of rotate and they don't set a starting lineup that often. In the fall they told me I would be starting."

"I was on the offensive staff at that time," said former Tigers assistant coach John Kadlec, "and we thought that when we recruited Wehrli that we were going to get him on offense. In the very first meeting, Coach Devine put Roger's tag on the personnel board on the defensive side, and boy, we started arguing.

Coach Devine said, 'That's the end of it. Roger is playing defense. We need speed on defense.'"

The 6-foot, 194-pound Wehrli provided just what Devine expected on defense. In 1968 he set a school single-season record with 7 interceptions, including another record 3 against Oklahoma State. He was selected as the Big Eight Defensive Player of the Year for his efforts.

Against Alabama in the 1969 Gator Bowl, Wehrli helped cement the Tigers' 35–10 victory. The Tigers held a 14–7 lead, but the Crimson Tide had the ball. Wehrli intercepted his second pass of the game at Alabama's 42 yard line and returned it to the 21. A few plays later, quarterback Terry McMillan ran for a 2-yard touchdown, giving Mizzou a comfortable margin.

Roger Wehrli's speed and quickness made Tigers coaches and opponents take notice.

As great as Wehrli was as a defensive back, he was even more dynamic as a kick returner. In the 1966 season opener against Iowa State, he returned the opening kickoff 96 yards for a touchdown in Mizzou's 23–7 victory. He victimized Iowa State again with six punt returns for 149 yards in 1968. Those returns set up four Missouri touchdowns in a 42–7 romp.

Twice Wehrli led the Tigers in punt returns (1966 and '68) and kickoff returns (1966 and '67). His 12-yard punt-return average led the nation in 1968. He holds school career records for punt returns (92) and for yards gained on punt returns in a game (156), season (478), and career (1,062).

"The biggest thrill was my records returning punts and kick-offs and making big plays," Wehrli said. "Certainly the interceptions and things like that are things you remember. I am proud of our strong defensive tradition throughout the sixties, and I'm proud to be part of that Devine era when Missouri football was well respected."

The St. Louis Cardinals knew enough about Wehrli's college exploits to make him a first-round draft choice in 1969. He played fourteen NFL seasons at one of football's most demanding positions and several years ago was ranked among the top 300 players in league history.

His 40 career interceptions are second on the Cardinals' all-time list to Pro Football Hall of Fame safety Larry Wilson. Wilson, who later became general manager of the Cardinals, said Wehrli is one of the greatest defensive backs he has ever seen. The seven-time Pro Bowl selection was forced to play a lot of man-for-man coverage because St. Louis used Wilson in a lot of blitz packages.

"There wasn't a better cornerback I played against," Pro Football Hall of Fame quarterback Roger Staubach told the *St. Louis Post-Dispatch*. "He was a great, great defensive back. You had to be aware of him all the time. Roger was a shut-down guy, absolutely. He was very smart. You would try to look him off, but obviously he could read what was taking place in the backfield. And you could tell he could read routes because he would always be there a step ahead. There's no question he should be in the [Pro Football] Hall of Fame."

The Prototype: All-America Tight End Kellen Winslow

Kellen Winslow played only one season of football at East St. Louis High School. That was all the rangy receiver needed to catch the eye of coaches at Mizzou, which sat proudly just a little more than two hours west along I-70 from St. Louis.

"You could see he was a great athlete and he'd develop," said Tigers head coach Al Onofrio, who recruited Winslow and coached him from 1975 to 1977. "He had a great attitude, which is why he became great."

"I was just this kid walking around [high] school," said Winslow. "I had seen the University of Missouri on TV on Sunday morning on the *Al Onofrio Show*. I had no idea it was 120 miles from where I lived."

Struggling to fit in, Winslow almost left the Missouri campus at the end of the first semester of his sophomore year. However, legendary Tigers trainer Fred Wappel and then Big Eight commissioner Prentice Gautt, a former Tigers coach and administrator, would not let him. "[Wappel] came into my life and kicked me in the [rear] when I needed it," Winslow said.

Winslow made a dramatic turnaround, but that didn't translate into statistical success. He never totaled more than 100 receiving yards in any game or led the Tigers in receiving for a season during his career at Mizzou.

He caught 70 passes for 1,077 yards in three seasons. The most prominent highlight of his career was a 16-yard touchdown catch in the Tigers' 20–15 victory over LSU in the 1978 Liberty Bowl.

Mizzou All-Americans

1925 Ed Lindenmeyer, T

1939 Paul Christman, QB

1941 Darold Jenkins, C

1942 Bob Steuber, HB

1955 Harold Burnine, E

1960 Danny LaRose, E

1961 Ed Blaine, T

1962 Conrad Hitchler, E

1965 Johnny Roland, DB

1965 Francis Peay, T

1967 Russ Washington, T

1968 Roger Wehrli, DB

1969 Mike Carroll, G

1973 Scott Anderson, C

1975 Johnny Moseley, DB

1976 Henry Marshall, WR

1978 Morris Towns, T

1978 Kellen Winslow, TE

1980 Bill Whitaker, DB

1981 Brad Edelman, C

1981 Jeff Gaylord, DT

1983 Conrad Goode, T

1986 John Clay, T

1998 Devin West, RB

1999 Rob Riti, C

2000 Justin Smith, DE

However, that didn't prevent Winslow from earning consensus All-America honors as a senior and being named the Big Eight Male Athlete of the Year. Missouri proved to be an excellent springboard for even greater future success.

Rather than just catching passes, for which he had a natural talent, Winslow learned how to excel at all aspects of the game, and that enabled him to become the most versatile tight end in NFL history. The San Diego Chargers selected Winslow with the thirteenth overall choice in the 1979 NFL draft, and the rest is football history.

"It isn't often you get the best player in the draft without your team having the worst record," said then Chargers owner Gene Klein.

From 1979 to 1987 Winslow caught 541 passes for 6,741 yards and 45 touchdowns. By the time he retired, the five-time Pro Bowl selection ranked second on San Diego's all-time receiving list behind Pro Football Hall of Fame receiver Charlie Joiner. Winslow also stood ahead of receivers Wes Chandler, John Jefferson, and even another Hall of Famer, Lance Alworth.

Winslow was inducted into the Pro Football Hall of Fame in 1995 and was a member of the NFL's 75th Anniversary All-Time Team. But the defining moments in his professional career came during San Diego's incredible 41–38 overtime victory over Miami in a 1981 AFC Divisional Playoff Game. Not only did Winslow catch 13 passes for 166 yards in the contest, but he also blocked a 43-yard field goal attempt as time expired in regulation to send the game into overtime. Winslow was so exhausted after the game that his teammates helped carry him off the field.

"Kellen had a little mean streak," said Hall of Fame Chargers quarterback Dan Fouts. "He used to drive me nuts. We'd line him up against some guy about five-two and 106 pounds, I'd throw him a little hitch, and I'd expect him to run away from the guy. Kellen would lower his shoulder and try to bury him."

Who knows how much greater Winslow's impact might have been? In 1984 and 1985 he missed seventeen games after suffering a knee injury that also hastened the end to his NFL days. He returned to play in 1986 and 1987 and even earned selection to the Pro Bowl in 1987, which proved to be his final game.

There is another postscript to Winslow's NFL career. In 1979 the Chargers had engineered a draft-day trade with the Cleveland Browns to select Winslow. Amazingly, the Cleveland Browns, unwilling to repeat the mistake, rebuffed multiple trade offers from other teams and chose tight end Kellen Winslow, Jr., with the sixth pick overall in the 2004 NFL draft.

Godzilla Storms Columbia: All-America Defensive End Justin Smith

When Notre Dame called to tell Jefferson City High School football star Justin Smith that they were interested in him, the university representative asked Smith how it felt to be courted by the football powerhouse. The 6-foot 5-inch, 256-pound defensive end, who had just led the Jays to a Missouri state high school championship, answered the rep with a chuckle.

Smith, who was also being courted by Nebraska and Miami, wasn't your average *SuperPrep* All-American. Raised on a farm in Holts Summitt, Missouri, Smith was a demon on the football field, but indifferent to the game off it.

The University of Missouri, which played to Smith's down-to-earth personality and disdain for bright lights and big cities, would suit him just fine. Adding to Mizzou's allure was the fact that Smith's parents, a sister, his grandfather, and several aunts had earned an education in Columbia. Tigers coaches also promised Smith he could start as a freshman. It didn't take Smith long to prove that the coaches had made a smart choice.

"I've only known a couple of players who could come in right away and dominate the way Justin did," said then Tigers head coach Larry Smith after Justin Smith's freshman season. "Justin's just starting to scratch the surface. Everything he does is based on natural ability. Once he learns technique, he's going to be that much better." The players Larry Smith was referring to were linebacker Junior Seau and defensive end Willie McGinest, both of whom he had coached at the University of Southern California.

"He has a tremendous nose for the ball, and he just goes and makes plays," Larry Smith added. "Some of that you can't teach. He has great quickness and great strength—he throws people around like rag dolls."

After becoming the first Missouri freshman to start every game since 1986 and earning Big Eight Defensive Freshman of the Year honors, Justin Smith proceeded to cement his legend at Mizzou—on the field and in the weight room. In fact, Smith, who developed arms as big as most people's legs through rigorous workouts, concerned Tigers coaches by spending *too* much time training. He holds the school record in the power clean.

"I see football as a test of manhood, and when I'm out on the field I'll do anything to win," Smith told *Sports Illustrated*.

Twice during his freshman season (in Tigers victories over

West Virginia in the Insight.com Bowl and Colorado), the man—nicknamed Godzilla because of his dominating presence—didn't even worry about whom to tackle on option plays. He just tackled both the quarterback and the running back.

"Sometimes when he sheds a blocker, I just don't know how he gets away with it, how he does it so easily," said teammate Danny McCamy after Smith's freshman season.

Smith tied for the team lead with 3.5 sacks as a freshman, tied a school record with a team-leading 8 sacks as a sophomore, and shattered the mark with 11 sacks as a junior. His 22.5 career sacks are an all-time record at Mizzou.

After Smith's junior season (in which he also led the Tigers with 97 tackles, including 24 tackles for a loss), the first-team All-America and All–Big Eight player decided to leave school for the NFL. Although the Tigers were more than disappointed to see him go, Smith, who ran the 40 in 4.6 seconds and was one of college football's fastest and strongest pass rushers, again made the right decision.

"I definitely made the right move," he said. "I came out the other side smelling like a rose and things turned out great." The Cincinnati Bengals made Smith the fourth overall pick in the 2001 NFL draft, and he joined Tigers tackle Russ Washington (San Diego, 1968) as the highest drafted players in Missouri history.

"He's a quick, agile, big guy," said Bengals head coach Dick LeBeau after the team drafted him. "So you have to figure our percentages just got better getting off the field on third down."

Cincinnati has built its defense around Smith, who established a team rookie record with 8.5 sacks in 2001. Through 2004

Legends

Eleven members of Missouri's football program are in the
National Football Foundation Hall of Fame.

1909	Bill Roper, coach
1919–20	Ed "Brick" Travis, T
1920–21	James Phelan, coach
1927–29	John Waldorf, official
1935–56	Don Faurot, player-coach
1938–40	Paul Christman, QB
1940–42	Bob Steuber, HB
1940–41	Darold Jenkins, C
1957	Frank Broyles, coach
1958–70	Dan Devine, coach
1962–65	Johnny Roland, DB

he had started 55 consecutive games for the Bengals and posted 26 sacks. He led the team in sacks and tackles among defensive linemen three times.

During his rookie season, Smith also intercepted two passes. The first interception came in a victory over Detroit and the second set up the first of two Bengals' touchdowns in the fourth quarter of a 26–23 overtime victory over the Pittsburgh Steelers.

Really Big Bowls

The Missouri Tigers have a rich history in bowl games, beginning with a cross-country road trip to southern California to face the USC Trojans in a 1924 Christmas Festival game. The 1960s proved to be the most illustrious decade for Mizzou in bowl games, including the school's first postseason victory—a 21–14 decision over Navy in the 1961 Orange Bowl.

Overall, the Tigers have played into December and January twenty-two times. They have made four appearances in the Orange Bowl, and their 20–18 win over Florida in the 1966 Sugar Bowl headlines their two Sugar Bowl stops.

Missouri has faced some of college football's greatest quarterbacks in the season's biggest games. Fran Tarkenton, who eventually earned induction into the Pro Football Hall of Fame, led Georgia against the Tigers in the 1960 Orange Bowl. Two other quarterbacks now in the Pro Football Hall of Fame, SMU's Bobby Layne and BYU's Steve Young, proved to be worthy opponents for Mizzou in the 1946 Cotton Bowl and 1983 Holiday Bowl, respectively. It was Young's 14-yard touchdown reception that gave his Cougars a 21–17 victory over the Tigers.

The Tigers' bowl games boast many memorable team and personal highlights. Who could forget Norm Beal's 90-yard interception return for a touchdown against Navy in the 1961 Orange Bowl or Carlos Posey's 70-yard touchdown return of a blocked field goal in a 34–31 victory over West Virginia in the 1998 Insight.com Bowl?

Several Tigers hold NCAA Bowl records. Mike Fink logged 203 total kickoff return yards and a 100-yard return against Arizona State in the 1972 Fiesta Bowl. And Bobby Bell sacked Steve Young a record four times in the 1983 Holiday Bowl.

In the 1968 Gator Bowl, Missouri mounted one of the most dominating team performances in NCAA history. The Tigers held Bear Bryant's Crimson Tide to minus-45 rushing yards, the fewest ever allowed. Missouri running back Greg Cook added a Tigers bowl-record 179 rushing yards in the 35–10 victory.

Sometimes a bowl victory can help change a program's fortunes, and Missouri's 1998 win over West Virginia provided a much-needed boost. Corby Jones tied a school record with 3 touchdowns as the Tigers defeated a team led by quarterback Marc Bulger, who went on to start for the St. Louis Rams. In 2003 Brad Smith set school bowl records with 17 completions in 30 passing attempts, and he gained 251 yards of total offense.

Bowl games don't measure the entire worth of a college football program. But the legends and memories they produce live on forever.

Near Perfection: 1961 Orange Bowl

If the 1961 Orange Bowl were held today, the Missouri Tigers not only would be playing for the first bowl victory in school history, they also would be competing for a first-ever national title. In the 1960s the college national champion was chosen before the bowl games were played.

Missouri entered the last week of the 1960 regular season as the only undefeated team in the country and ranked first in the national polls. A demoralizing 23–7 loss to Kansas, which used an ineligible player in the game and later would have to forfeit the victory, gave the Big Ten champion University of Minnesota, also with just one loss, the national title.

The 1961 Orange Bowl marked the second consecutive year— and the third time overall—the Tigers had traveled to Miami on January 1. The first two Orange Bowl trips ended with a 21–7 loss to Georgia Tech in 1940 and a 14–0 loss to Georgia. The third time proved to be the charm as Mizzou, powered by running backs Mel West (108 rushing yards) and Donnie Smith (93), defeated Navy

Man of Steel

Dan Devine led the Tigers to national prominence and three Orange Bowls in the 1960s behind the stellar performances of players like Andy Russell. Devine knew how to lure top-notch talent, and the rangy 6-foot 3-inch star was an especially big fish.

Russell was a high school star in the upscale neighborhood of Ladue, just outside of St. Louis. As a senior, Russell (whose father was a Harvard graduate and business executive) seemed destined for an Ivy League school, but Devine wooed Russell and his parents to Missouri by showing them the library, emphasizing the school's high academic standards, and inviting prominent people from around the state to extol the virtues of being a Tiger.

Russell proved to be a multidimensional player at Missouri. As a fullback, he led the Tigers with 412 rushing yards on 100 carries in 1961. As a linebacker, he led the team with six interceptions in 1962 and was a team captain. In Mizzou's 20–14 victory over Navy in the 1961 Orange Bowl, Russell intercepted two passes.

As good as Russell was with the Tigers, he was even better as a linebacker for the Pittsburgh Steelers. Not that big or fast, Russell was known as the thinking man's linebacker in twelve NFL seasons.

Russell won two world championships with the Steelers, who captured Super Bowls IX and X. Russell intercepted eighteen passes and scored two touchdowns during his NFL career.

"You don't fool Andy," said Steelers coach Chuck Noll. "He's about the best I've seen at reading a play and getting to the right place at the right time."

and Heisman Trophy–winning running back Joe Bellino 21–14.

President-elect John F. Kennedy, a former Naval officer, was on hand to cheer on the Midshipmen. What Kennedy saw in the first quarter was a frantic exchange of big plays. Missouri drove to Navy's 2 yard line only to fumble and see Midshipman Greg Mather return it 98 yards for the game's first score.

The extra point failed, and Navy had a 6–0 lead. The Tigers answered with a school bowl-record 90-yard interception return from Norm Beal to take a lead that they would never relinquish.

Missouri, which rushed for 296 yards to Navy's minus-8 during the game, pushed its advantage to 21–6 on a 4-yard touchdown run by Smith and a 1-yard run from Ron Taylor. Bellino scored the final points of the game on a 27-yard touchdown reception.

The Tigers lost a school bowl-record five fumbles but offset those miscues by intercepting four Navy passes (two by sophomore linebacker Andy Russell, one by Beal, and one by Fred Brossart on the game's final play).

"That was a big thrill," Russell said in *Tales from the Missouri Tigers* by Alan Goforth. "The President of the United States was up in the stands rooting for Navy. They had the Heisman Trophy winner, Joe Bellino, but we shut him down. That was the highlight, which happened in my sophomore year."

Mizzou finished fourth in the UPI poll and fifth in the AP poll. Ultimately, Minnesota lost to UCLA in the Rose Bowl while Missouri's victory would have given the Tigers the national championship. In a bit of irony, the Tigers traveled to Minneapolis for the opening game of the 1961 season and defeated the Gophers 6–0.

Missouri captured the Orange Bowl trophy on its third try. The Tigers defeated Navy 21–14.

Sweet Victory: 1966 Sugar Bowl

Mizzou used a powerful, ball-control rushing attack to keep Heisman Trophy–winning quarterback Steve Spurrier off the field and defeat the University of Florida 20–18 in the 1966 Sugar Bowl. Of their 76 total plays, the Tigers, who won their third consecutive bowl game under head coach Dan Devine, ran the ball 62 times, piling up a 257-yard to minus-2-yard advantage on the ground.

Missouri had the nation's third-ranked rushing offense. For the first time in school history, the Tigers also featured two first-team All-Americans—tackle Francis Peay and defensive back Johnny Roland—on the same team.

On the first series of the game, Mizzou marched 71 yards in 18 plays, but Florida stopped Tigers fullback Carl Reese cold on fourth-and-one at the Gators' 9 yard line. Florida went three-and-out, and Missouri responded with a 13-play, 59-yard drive that ended with a 10-yard touchdown run by Charlie Brown, who finished with a game-high 120 rushing yards.

The Gators went three-and-out again on the next series and then fumbled a punt return that led to an 11-yard touchdown pass from Roland to Earl Denny. A Spurrier fumble and interception and a botched fake punt also helped keep Florida at bay through the first three quarters. The Tigers led 20–0 as the fourth quarter began.

The Gators put on an offensive fireworks show in the final stanza, but it was not enough. Showing why he was selected as the nation's top player, Spurrier threw touchdown passes of 22 and 21 yards and ran for a 2-yard score to narrow the gap to 20–18.

Mizzou's defense, which was ranked eighth in the country, may not have been able to stop the game's eventual MVP from producing three touchdowns (Spurrier set Sugar Bowl records with 27 completions in 46 attempts for 352 yards), but it did stop the Gators on all three of their 2-point conversion tries.

"The fans saw two great football teams today," Devine said after the game. "Either Florida or Missouri could have played with any team in the country. Florida made two fine defensive stands. Spurrier is a great football player, always dangerous."

The Tigers finished the 1965 season with an 8–2–1 record and a sixth-place ranking in the national polls.

Legendary Upset: 1968 Gator Bowl

The Missouri Tigers' 35–10 victory over the Alabama Crimson Tide in the 1968 Gator Bowl was not as close as the score suggested. In securing the most dominating bowl victory in Mizzou history, the Tigers rushed for school bowl-record 402 yards while limiting the Crimson Tide to minus-45 yards on the ground.

"They ran through us like we were a barber's college," legendary Alabama head coach Paul "Bear" Bryant lamented after the game.

Missouri had lost its final two games of the 1968 season to sixth-ranked Oklahoma and seventh-ranked Kansas and came into the Gator Bowl with a 7–3 record. The heavily favored Crimson Tide had won a national title two seasons earlier and were ranked twelfth in the nation.

"Bear Bryant said before the game—and he said this very seldom—that that was the best defensive team he had in a long time,"

The Gator Bowl was the site for one of Missouri's greatest triumphs on the football field—a 35-10 victory over the Alabama Crimson Tide.

then Tigers defensive coordinator Al Onofrio said in *Tales from the Missouri Tigers*. "They had a great passer and a good offense, and they ended up minus-45 yards for the game. Our running backs made an awful lot of yards. We completely dominated the game."

In a harbinger of things to come, Missouri running back Greg Cook swept around the right side for 33 yards on the first play of the game. Ten plays later, Tigers quarterback Terry McMillan ran 4 yards to give Mizzou a 7–0 lead.

Alabama made a first down on its first two plays, but after three more plays the Crimson Tide was forced to punt. On its next four series, Alabama went three plays and out. The Crimson Tide would finish the game by going three-and-out eight of the thirteen times they had the ball. Only a Missouri pass interference penalty kept that from being nine of thirteen.

However, a 38-yard interception return by Alabama's Donnie Sutton evened the score at 7–7. McMillan scored on a 5-yard run to give Missouri a 14–7 halftime lead.

A fumble by All-American Roger Wehrli and another interception by McMillan allowed the Crimson Tide to narrow the gap to 14–10 early in the fourth quarter. The Tigers, who had spent the week training in Daytona Beach, were fresh, and Wehrli's 21-yard interception return led to McMillan's third touchdown.

Cook, who set a school bowl-record with 179 rushing yards, followed McMillan's score with a 36-yard touchdown run. Dennis Poppe returned an interception 47 yards for the game's final touchdown. McMillan was selected as the game's MVP.

"It was a great way to end my career at Missouri," All-America cornerback Roger Wehrli, who was married before the game and celebrated his honeymoon during the trip to Daytona Beach, told the *Columbia Missourian*. "I look back, and that's the thing I remember."

"It might have been the biggest defeat ever for a Bear Bryant team, but after the game he was very complimentary toward me and our team," wrote Missouri head coach Dan Devine in his autobiography. "He was very kind to my family, and we developed a very nice friendship which continued for years."

Cooked Cajuns: 1978 Liberty Bowl

Warren Powers inherited a talent-laden team when he took over as Missouri's head coach in 1978. Led by quarterback Phil

Bradley, tight end Kellen Winslow, running back James Wilder, linemen Pete Allard and Kurt Peterson, defensive backs Russ Calabrese, Eric Wright, Johnnie Poe, and Bill Whitaker, and linebacker Chris Garlich, the Tigers and Powers never had to look far when they needed a big play.

It seemed as if every member of Missouri's star-studded cast got into the act in an impressive 20–15 victory over LSU in the 1978 Liberty Bowl.

The Tigers' offense dominated the first half. On the first series of the game, the sophomore Bradley guided Mizzou on a 75-yard drive that culminated with a 13-yard run around end by running back Earl Grant.

Three series later, Bradley tossed a 16-yard touchdown pass to Winslow. Wilder, who was named the game's most valuable player after rushing for 115 yards, put the Tigers ahead 20–3 with a punishing 3-yard touchdown run right before halftime.

Overall, Missouri amassed 223 total yards and 14 first downs on offense in the first half. Mizzou finished the game with 317 total yards and 18 first downs.

"I can't say that Missouri is the most physical team we've played," said LSU head coach Charlie McClendon in a postgame interview, "but that quarterback Bradley is some kind of quarterback. He's really a good player, and he showed a lot of maturity out there tonight."

The second half provided a showcase for Missouri's defense. LSU cut the Tigers' lead to 20–9 with a 1-yard run by All-America running back Charles Alexander that capped an 80-yard drive on the opening series of the second half. The LSU offense also included quarterback David Woodley and receiver Carlos Carson, both of whom eventually would join Alexander as solid players in the NFL.

Missouri's defense rebounded from the score with a blocked extra point by Peterson, an interception by Whitaker, a forced fumble by Norman Goodman with LSU on Missouri's 25 yard line, and an interception by Peterson. Overall, the Black and Gold's defense forced five LSU turnovers (four interceptions and a forced fumble).

"It was a team game, a team victory," said Eric Berg, who had an interception and a fumble recovery, after the game. "Our offense came out and just exploded for those 20 points. Then, when they got the momentum, we knew we had to come up from somewhere to stop 'em on defense."

"That's the way a team is supposed to work," said Winslow. "When one doesn't do it, the other has to."

Insight into the Future: 1998 Insight.com Bowl

As they prepared to face the University of West Virginia in the 1998 Insight.com Bowl, the Missouri Tigers had not won a post-season game since defeating Southern Mississippi 19–17 in the 1981 Tangerine Bowl. The Tigers had defeated the Golden Eagles by limiting their versatile quarterback Reggie Collier—the first signal caller in NCAA Division I history to gain more than 1,000 yards rushing and passing, respectively, in the same season—to 16 yards on the ground and 54 through the air.

In 1998 it was Missouri that had the double-threat quarterback. One season earlier, Corby Jones had set a school single-season record with 2,545 yards total offense (887 rushing and

1,658 passing). Jones finished his collegiate career as the Tigers' all-time leader with 38 rushing touchdowns and 64 total touchdowns (38 rushing and 26 passing).

Not only did the Mountaineers have to face Jones's athletic ability, they also had to overcome an extremely motivated player who had lost his father, Curtis, a Missouri assistant coach, to a heart attack before the season began. Corby Jones was as good as advertised, tying an Insight.com and Missouri bowl record with three rushing touchdowns as the Tigers defeated West Virginia 34–31.

Another Jones—sophomore cornerback Julian, who was starting in place of conference interception leader Wade Perkins, who had been suspended for violating team rules—played an equally impressive role. Julian had ten tackles, intercepted a pass, blocked a punt for a safety, returned the ensuing kick 34 yards to help set up a touchdown, and was named the game's MVP.

"There's not much you can say," said Corby. "We just did this for my dad and for the team."

Plays on special teams, including a 70-yard return of a blocked field goal for a touchdown and a 60-yard kickoff return that set up a touchdown, helped stake Missouri to a 31–10 lead late in the third quarter. However, three of the Tigers' losses during the regular season had come after blowing halftime leads.

"Those three losses, we came out of there angry and upset," said then Tigers head coach Larry Smith, "because we knew we could play those people nose-to-nose. But a mistake here and a mistake there, and we get beat. We didn't want to let that happen this game. There was a lot of hunger to win."

Led by quarterback Marc Bulger, who completed 34 of 51 passes (both Insight.com Bowl records) for 429 yards and 4 second-half

"The Tackle"

The Hail Mary. The Ghost to the Post. The Music City Miracle. Some moments live forever in NFL history. One such indelible moment took place on the final play of Super Bowl XXXIV, when St. Louis Rams running back (and former Missouri Tiger) Mike Jones made "The Tackle."

With less than two minutes remaining in the game, the Rams led the Tennessee Titans 23–16. Things looked bleak for the Titans, but quarterback Steve McNair coolly directed Tennessee down the field, and with 6 seconds left the Titans had the ball on the Rams' 10 yard line. Tennessee called Z Sliver, in which Titans tight end Frank Wycheck and receiver Kevin Dyson lined up on the right side of the line. Wycheck would run a seam route and Dyson a quick slant underneath the coverage.

St. Louis countered with a coverage called Trio. Jones, cornerback Todd Lyght, and safety Keith Lyle played a three-on-two defense against Dyson and Wycheck.

On the snap, Dyson ran 5 yards downfield before making his cut. "I saw him [Dyson] out of the corner of my eye," said Jones later. "I didn't see the ball, but I saw his eyes get big so I knew the ball was coming. . . . I couldn't see McNair throw the ball, but I could feel it."

Jones recovered to make the initial hit with Dyson around the 3 yard line. Jones clutched Dyson's left leg and foot, halting the lanky receiver's momentum. Then, with an incredible burst of second effort, Jones kept Dyson from getting to the goal line. Dyson's hand and the ball came to rest on the 1 yard line.

"All I saw was yellow paydirt," said Dyson. "I just couldn't get the nose of the ball over the goal line. When he [Jones] got his hands on me, I thought I was going to break the tackle. But he got my foot, tripped me up and wrapped up nice. He made a great play."

Mike Jones (52) came to Missouri as a running back, but he made his mark with one play as an NFL linebacker in Super Bowl XXXIV. Kevin Terrell

Super Tigers

Alphabetically, end Bud Abell is the first Missouri Tiger to play professional football. Abell also is the first Missouri alum to play in the Super Bowl, toiling for the Kansas City Chiefs in a 35–10 loss to the Green Bay Packers in Super Bowl I. The most decorated Super Bowl Tiger is cornerback Eric Wright, who started for the San Francisco 49ers in the 1980s and helped them win four Super Bowls. Following is a list of all Mizzou Tigers who have played in a Super Bowl:

Bud Abell, E, Chiefs (Participant in Super Bowl I)

Scott Anderson, C, Vikings (Participant in Super Bowl XI)

Ken Bungarda, T, 49ers (Super Bowl ring in XVI)

Byron Chamberlain, TE, Broncos (Super Bowl rings in XXXII and XXXIII)

Tony Galbreath, RB, Giants (Super Bowl ring in XXI)

Michael Jones, LB, Rams (Super Bowl ring in XXXIV)

Rick Lyle, DT, Patriots (Super Bowl ring in XXXVIII)

Damon Mays, WR, Steelers (Participant in Super Bowl XXX)

Larry Moss, RB, Steelers (Super Bowl ring in X)

A. J. Ofodile, TE, Steelers (Participant in Super Bowl XXX)

Gus Otto, LB, Raiders (Participant in Super Bowl II)

Andy Russell, LB, Steelers (Super Bowl rings in IX and X)

Jerome Sally, NT, Giants (Super Bowl ring in XXI)

Otis Smith, CB, Patriots (Super Bowl rings in XXXVI and XXXVIII)

Joe Stewart, WR, Raiders (Super Bowl ring in XV)

Henry Stuckey, DB, Dolphins (Super Bowl rings in VII and VIII)

Eric Wright, CB, 49ers (Super Bowl rings in XVI, XIX, XXIII, and XXIV) touchdowns, West Virginia cut Missouri's lead to 31–24 with a little more than ten minutes remaining. The Mountaineers had momentum, but the Tigers responded with one of the school's greatest drives.

Getting 46 rushing yards on 12 carries from senior running back Devin West, who had been selected as the Tigers' first All-American in twelve years, Missouri used nearly seven minutes on a fourteen-play drive that culminated with a field goal and a 34–24 advantage.

Mizzou senior safety Caldrinoff Easter described the drive as "rock-'em, sock-'em, in-your-face, smash-mouth football."

"They're probably the most mentally tough football team I've ever been around," said Smith, who had previously served as head coach at USC and Arizona. "We've had a lot of adversity, but you know what? Nobody complained; they just kept playing."

During the regular season, West finished fifth in the nation and broke Missouri's single-season rushing record with 1,578 yards. He finished the Insight.com Bowl with 125 yards in 31 attempts, outperforming the nation's sixth best runner, Amos Zereoue, who managed just 32 yards in 22 carries for West Virginia.

"I have to take my hat off to Missouri," Zereoue said. "They did a good job, and they capitalized on our mistakes. It was frustrating because I didn't get to do what I wanted. The defense was always there at the line."

The bowl victory allowed Missouri to finish with an 8–4 record, the school's best since finishing 8–4 in 1981. The Tigers were poised to begin reversing more than a decade of struggles on the gridiron.

"It's [the Missouri football program has] turned the corner, yes," said West after the game.

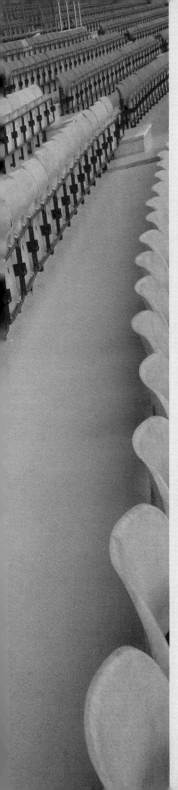

The Border War

Missouri versus Kansas is the oldest college football rivalry west of the Mississippi River, and for most of its 113 years it has been known simply as the Border War. The label "Border War" was not created to add marketing flair for the game. It finds its roots in one of the darkest hours of American history.

The official start of the American Civil War is commonly considered to have been April 12, 1861, when shots were fired at Fort

Sumter, South Carolina. However, almost a year earlier the "civil war" between Union and Confederate loyalists had already resulted in massive bloodshed along the border of Kansas and Missouri.

In response to raids on Missouri farmers by Jim Lane's and Doc Jennison's Jayhawkers, William Clarke Quantrill, who led the Bushwackers, a group of guerrilla fighters from Missouri, planned an attack on the city of Lawrence, Kansas. Quantrill and his men killed every man they saw (about 150), looted the town, and eventually burned it to the ground. Only women and children were left unharmed.

The 1999 movie *Ride with the Devil* offers a vivid recollection of the intense struggles along the Kansas-Missouri border during the early 1860s. It was a time that pitted neighbor against neighbor, family member against family member. Quantrill's sacking of Lawrence was one of the bloodiest battles of the Civil War and, according to history books, it brought the Border War to a climax.

When Missouri and Kansas first met on the neutral football field at Kansas City's Exposition Park in 1891, only two and a half decades had passed since the end of the Civil War. Old grudges were quickly rekindled, and the war was back on. The early years of the MU-KU football games were marred with fistfights, insults, and broken friendships and families.

"The hatred [of the wars] spilled right over into football," said Larry Smith, the Missouri Tigers' football coach from 1994 to 2000. "No one had to impress it [the importance of the rivalry with Kansas] upon me. In football and basketball here, it's real simple. It's KU. You don't have to take long to find that out. Just read the history and tradition."

Putting a hurt on Kansas
always brings a smile to the
faces of Missouri fans.

Mizzou's Most Wanted List

Anyone who played or coached at the University of Kansas: Does the rest of the list really matter to Tigers fans?

Kansas head coach Pepper Rodgers: Deserves special mention among all Jayhawks because of his ability to defeat and get under the skin of the legendary Dan Devine. Rodgers once gave Devine the peace sign after the game, and Devine purportedly returned the sign—minus his pointer finger.

Oklahoma head coach Bud Wilkinson: Figuratively "stole" Don Faurot's Split T formation and used it to do evil against his former mentor, winning three national titles and an NCAA-record forty-seven games.

Colorado head coach Bill McCartney: The former Mizzou player used five downs to beat the Tigers and went on to win the national championship in 1989.

Nebraska wide receiver Shevin Wiggins: Number-one-ranked Nebraska was facing sure defeat at the hands of Missouri in Columbia when Wiggins turned soccer star and "kicked" an errant pass to teammate Matt Davison in the end zone. Missouri lost in overtime.

Tigers defensive lineman John Matuszak: The fiery, 6-foot 8-inch, 295-pound Tooz got into a fight at a local night spot, was dismissed from the

More than 2,000 people showed up to watch the first Missouri-Kansas football game at Exposition Park. Missouri lost that game 22–10 and the second meeting 12–4. Despite the losses, Mizzou earned enough money from the games to keep its fledgling football program alive.

In 1893 H. O. Robinson, a star from Tufts College in Boston, enrolled as a student at Missouri and also was hired to coach the Tigers. He led Mizzou to its first victory over the Jayhawks in his first team, transferred to the University of Tampa, and ended up the number-one overall selection in the 1973 NFL draft. Oh, what might have been had the Tooz not lost his cool!

Arkansas head football coach and athletic director Frank Broyles: Handpicked by Faurot to replace himself as the Tigers' head football coach, Broyles spent one season in Columbia before bolting for a more lucrative deal with the Razorbacks. So much for loyalty (and this was in 1956). Broyles would have been higher on this list had Devine not replaced him.

Ohio State University: From 1939 to 1949 the Tigers faced the Buckeyes nine times in either the first or second game of each respective season. Even with Faurot at the helm for six of those games, the best Mizzou could do was earn one tie.

Oklahoma coach Barry Switzer: Isn't the bootlegger's son on everyone's list, especially in the Big 12 Conference?

BYU, Georgia, Maryland, Miami (Florida), Oregon State, Pittsburgh, Stanford, Syracuse, Temple, Tulane, UCLA: Between these schools Missouri is a combined 0-25-3. At least Tulane, which is 0-0-2, can't say it beat the Tigers.

season. However, Robinson missed the train to the Kansas game the following season, and the Tigers' 18–12 loss cost him his job.

Along with the emotional toll, there was a significant financial cost to watch the rivalry, even during it infancy. In 1895 a $1.00 ticket got fans a seat to watch the Tigers defeat Kansas 10–6. Other games on the roster cost 25 cents.

In 1896 Missouri fans paid $3.50 to travel round-trip from Columbia to Kansas City to witness the Jayhawks' 30–0 thrashing of the Tigers. Kansas lost 12–0 to Mizzou in 1898, the same year a snow-covered field had to be lined by black charcoal.

At the turn of the century, the number of fans attending the rivalry game had risen to 8,000, and they were able to see Missouri and Kansas kiss each other for the first time with a 6–6 tie. Ernie Quigly, who would become a renowned major league baseball umpire, provided most of the fireworks. The reserve Kansas halfback returned a punt 65 yards for a touchdown and chased down Missouri's Charley Webster from behind as he rambled toward the end zone on a 50-yard run.

The Tigers' record against Kansas from 1891 to 1908 was 3–13–2, including a seven-game winless streak between 1898 and 1908. Mizzou, which had fired its previous coaches mostly because they couldn't beat the Jayhawks, finally turned the tide in the rivalry with the hiring of former Princeton star William W. Roper as head coach in 1909. A 12–6 victory on Thanksgiving Day gave Missouri the only undefeated season in its history.

The Missouri-Kansas rivalry has been filled with exciting moments, including one orchestrated by 145-pound back Russell Dills, who broke open a 25–6 victory in 1928 with a 100-yard kickoff return for a touchdown. The *Kansas City Star* later described Dills as "a dancing sunbeam, whirling like a Hindu dervish, with his shadowy jigstep."

Missouri's worst defeat in rivalry history was a 32–0 pounding in 1929. The victory propelled the Jayhawks, led by All-America back and Olympic decathlete Jim Bausch, to the Big Six Conference title. However, Mizzou refused to go quietly. W. A. Tarr, a faculty rep at Missouri, questioned Bausch's amateur status. Late in the season, the Big Six faculty representatives issued the following statement: "In view of the practices at the University of Kansas in violating the rule of this conference relating to recruiting and subsidizing athletes, the other five members of this conference decline to schedule any athletic games, not now under contract, with the University of Kansas." The Big Six eventually reinstated Kansas.

Entering the 2005 college football season, the all-time record in the Missouri-Kansas rivalry stood at 52–52–9. The feeling elicited by a tie game has been compared to kissing your sister. Well, the Missouri-Kansas matchup has been so even that it's become more like kissing all of your female relatives.

The rivalry didn't start so balanced. Kansas had twenty-three victories and four ties in its first forty-two meetings with the Tigers. From 1925 to 1934, the Jayhawks had a 7–3 mark against their neighbors.

All of that changed when Don Faurot was hired in 1935. Mizzou played to a 0–0 tie with Kansas in Faurot's first season, and over the next seven years the Tigers were 6–0–1.

From 1943 to 1945 Faurot left the Missouri sidelines for World War II. When he returned to Columbia in 1946, he lost two consecutive games against the Jayhawks, but won seven of his next nine contests with his archrival. Overall, Faurot had a 13–4–2 record against Kansas. Only Dan Devine (9–2–2) had a better winning percentage (with a minimum of at least two games).

Faurot's most memorable game against Kansas probably was his final game as the Tigers' head football coach. Before the 1956 college season, Faurot had announced it would be his final one on the Missouri sidelines. The team did not play well and had a

Slippery Ice and a Road Grader

In 1941 Missouri's 155-pound halfback Harry "Slippery" Ice lived up to his nickname by shredding the Jayhawks' defense for 240 rushing yards on only eight carries. Missouri won that game, which was played in a rainstorm that turned into a second-half snowstorm, 45–6—then the most lopsided victory over Kansas in Tigers history.

On September 13, 1998—fifty-seven years after Ice's remarkable game—Devin West, a 6-foot 2-inch, 227-pound senior running back in his first season as a full-time starter, propelled the twenty-fifth-ranked Tigers

to a 41–23 victory over the Jayhawks. West carried the ball thirty-three times for a record 319 yards, helping Mizzou (a 17-point favorite) overcome two deficits for the win.

"That was a fantastic performance," said Tigers head coach Larry Smith following West's performance. "I've coached a lot of years and had a lot of great backs, and I swear that I've never had one that gave that kind of effort."

All-American Devin West battered the Jayhawks with 319 rushing yards in 1998.

3–5–1 record entering its Homecoming game with the Jayhawks. A week before Homecoming, the Tigers had been humiliated 67–14 by Oklahoma.

Homecoming festivities turned into a tribute to Faurot. Kansas controlled most of the game and led 13–7 late in the fourth quarter. Missouri had moved the ball to the Jayhawks' 14 yard line when backup quarterback Dave Doane avoided an almost certain sack and tossed a touchdown pass to end Larry Plumb. An extra point would give the Tigers the lead; however, the snap on the point-after attempt was bad, and Missouri couldn't convert the kick.

A tie seemed certain until Kansas coach Chuck Mather made a huge mistake. With less than a minute to play in the game and the ball on his own 4 yard line, Mather inexplicably called for a reverse. Mizzou's Chuck Mehrer read the reverse perfectly and tackled Bobby Robinson in the end zone for a safety, and the Tigers won 15–13.

Missouri fans stormed the field, tore down the goal posts, and gave Faurot a standing ovation. Faurot's players carried the legendary coach off the field and into the sunset on their shoulders.

The euphoria of that victory was countered by the despair of a gut-wrenching loss four years later.

In the movie *The Outlaw Josey Wales*, Clint Eastwood plays a Missouri farmer who utters the phrase, "There's three kinds of sons in Kansas: Sunshine. Sunflowers. And mostly sons-of-bitches!" The Border War aside, most Missourians have never forgiven the Jayhawks for what they did on November 19, 1960.

Missouri entered its yearly battle against Kansas ranked number one in the nation, riding the wave of a 9–0 record, and sport-

In 1960 the Tigers were seemingly outnumbered at every turn against rival Kansas. However, the Jayhawks ultimately had to forfeit their victory.

ing a 41–19 victory over Oklahoma a week earlier. It was the Tigers' first win over the Sooners in twenty-four years.

The Jayhawks, led by quarterback John Hadl and backs Curtis McClinton and Bert Coan, were a good team, but they could not play in a bowl game because of earlier recruiting infractions. Missouri had everything to lose, and Kansas had nothing to lose—a recipe for disaster.

"It was the most exciting thing I've seen in my life," former Tigers head coach Woody Widenhofer, who was on Missouri's freshman team in 1960, told the *St. Louis Post-Dispatch* in 1985.

"They had a great football team themselves and we were ranked number one in the nation."

A record crowd of 43,000 at Mizzou's Memorial Stadium saw the Tigers lose 23–7. Coan scored two touchdowns in the game, and Kansas held Missouri's potent offense to 114 yards total offense and 186 below the Tigers' season average.

Tigers head coach Dan Devine, who would lose only twice to the Jayhawks in thirteen games, shouldered the blame for the loss, saying that he pushed the players too hard the week before the game and allowed too many distractions.

Missouri freshmen, who guarded the goal posts in a tradition that dated back to Faurot's days, kept Kansas fans from tearing down the apparatus after the game. Despite the crushing loss, the Tigers won the Big Eight Conference title and accepted a berth to the Orange Bowl. Against Heisman Trophy–winner Joe Bellino and Navy, Missouri won 21–14 and finished the season ranked fifth in the Associated Press poll—the highest final AP ranking in school history.

What made the 1960 defeat to Kansas especially painful was the fact that the NCAA later ruled Coan ineligible because he had accepted a free flight to a college all-star game from a KU alumnus. Kansas was forced to forfeit the game, so technically Missouri finished 11–0, instead of 10–1.

"That defeat was a bitter one," Al Onofrio was quoted in the *St. Louis Post-Dispatch* in 2003. "When you lose, you lose . . . but we would've had a chance at the national championship."

Missouri has played Kansas eleven times when the Tigers have been nationally ranked and the Jayhawks have not. The Tigers' record in those games is 7–4, including the forfeit victory

Big Plays in the Big Game

Of course, when you're the longest-playing rivalry west of the Mississippi, your odds of posting records on the football field increase dramatically. But that doesn't take away from the fact: Mizzou football has recorded some amazing stats against the Kansas Jayhawks.

In 1964 the Tigers tied a school record with 0 penalties in a 34–14 decision. The impressive part of this record is that it's happened only twice in school history (the first time was against Oklahoma in 1943).

Missouri recovered a record 8 fumbles against KU in 1950. However, the Tigers were just evening the score, having lost a record 7 fumbles to the Jayhawks a year earlier.

In 1949 MU ran a record 105 offensive plays against Kansas.

In 1969 MU set a team record with 4 touchdown passes in a game against KU. The Tigers equaled the mark in 1989.

The Tigers set a single-game record by scoring 69 points against the Jayhawks in 1969.

Missouri's Vince Turner returned a fumble a record 103 yards for a touchdown in 1963.

Russell Dills set a MU record with a 100-yard kickoff return for a touchdown in 1928.

In 1989 quarterback Kent Kiefer set a Tigers record with 444 passing yards. However, the Tigers lost a heartbreaker 46–44. Three years later, Jeff Handy eclipsed Kiefer's mark with 480 passing yards in a 28–26 defeat at Oklahoma State.

Mizzou defeated Kansas 31–21 in Lawrence one year after Kiefer's brilliant performance. Freshman Phil Johnson passed for 309 yards, and 229 of those went to Linzy Collins, who set the school's single-game receiving yards mark. Collins accounted for 193 of Kiefer's total in 1989.

Forty-one times during school history a Tigers runner has gained more than 150 rushing yards in a game. Eleven of those performances have come against the Jayhawks.

from 1960. Kansas has a 2–2 record against the Tigers when it was the only ranked team. Only twice have both teams been ranked when they played, and the Jayhawks won the Indian drum both times.

The roots of the Indian drum date to 1935. Kansas had won five games in a row from 1930 to 1934, and the Tigers had lost those games by a combined score of 100–0. In an attempt to restore black and gold passion for the game and add even more importance to the outcome, a couple of Missouri alumni came up with the idea of presenting an Indian drum to the winner of the 1935 game.

They chose the Indian drum to honor the Osage Indians who had roamed both the Kansas and Missouri plains. Legend has it that the original drum was purchased in a Kansas City pawnshop, and a replacement drum was purchased in 1986. The first Indian Drum game was a 0–0 tie, but Missouri's fortunes changed after Don Faurot arrived on the scene in 1935.

Devine Times

The Vietnam War . . . drugs . . . free love . . . The 1960s were a decade of strife, protests, and struggle throughout the United States. However, one haven from all the confusion existed in Columbia, Missouri. The 1960s were divine—or Devine, as in head coach Dan Devine—for the Missouri Tigers football program.

From 1958 to 1970 Devine put together the greatest string of football seasons that Mizzou fans have ever witnessed. During the six-

ties Missouri was the only NCAA Division I program to avoid losing more than three games in a season, and only seven schools
had a higher winning percentage in the decade than the Tigers'
.762 (77–22–6).

"Dan Devine was a winner, and he knew how to get players
to play," said Hank Kuhlman, who played one season for Devine
and eventually served as Devine's assistant for fifteen more. "He
was loved by his football players. He also knew how to delegate
authority. He was a disciplinarian. He made his teams do what
they needed to do. He was a very good, loyal person, and he
turned Missouri into a winner."

In all, Devine posted a 93–37–7 record and eight top-twenty-
five national rankings in thirteen seasons at Missouri. He guided
the Tigers to the Orange Bowl (three times), Sugar Bowl, Gator
Bowl, and Bluebonnet Bowl, winning four of the six games—the
highest bowl game winning percentage among all coaches in MU
history. Devine's bowl game record most likely would have been
even more impressive had the Tigers players not voted against
going to bowl games following the 1961, '66, and '67 seasons.

"It wasn't that long a time that he spent at Missouri, a total of
fifteen years," said University of Oklahoma athletic director Joe
Castiglione, who served as Missouri's athletic director from 1994 to
1998. "But the mystique, the aura, the way people responded to
him, most people would think that he spent his entire life there."

Following the 1957 season, in which he led Arizona State to
a perfect record, Devine was invited to speak at the National
Football Coaches Association meeting in New York. The president of the association was Don Faurot. After returning to
Phoenix following the meetings, Devine received a message that

During Dan Devine's thirteen-year tenure as Missouri's head football coach, the Tigers posted ninety-three victories and appeared in six bowl games, winning four.

Faurot wanted to discuss the head coaching position at Missouri.

Devine's first visit to Missouri almost became his last. The plane from Phoenix to Kansas City had to stop to refuel, and Devine arrived in Kansas at 1 A.M. During the flight, a woman spilled a cup of hot chocolate all over Devine—and the only suit he had brought for the interview.

In what could have been a scene in the movie *Planes, Trains, and Automobiles*, it was very cold when Devine arrived in Missouri, and he wasn't dressed for the weather. Faurot picked up Devine from the airport and, midway along the two-and-a-half-hour drive between Kansas City and Columbia, Faurot's car ran out of gas. While Faurot hitched a ride with a trucker to get gas, Devine sat shivering alone in the car, wondering why he ever made the trip.

Fortunately for Tigers fans, Devine, then thirty-three years old, was so impressed with Faurot—who the trucker greeted with the question, "What do you want, Don?"—and the Mizzou boosters that he decided to take the job of turning Missouri into a national power.

"He wasn't born here," former Kansas City Tiger Club president Paul Blackman said after Devine's death in 2002. "He didn't die here. But he was Missouri through and through. I think he epitomized the state, what was best of it."

Devine was born in western Wisconsin in 1924, but times were tough and his parents didn't have the means to care for him. His aunt and uncle raised him in Proctor, Minnesota, part of the state's rugged Iron Range.

There was no running water at Devine's childhood home, and a simple kerosene stove battled the harsh Minnesota winters. If any of Devine's seven children ever complained about how tough they had things, he could tell the story—without a snicker—about how he had to walk uphill for miles in 40-below temperatures to get to school.

In 1942 Devine left Proctor for the Army Air Corps. He trained to serve on the crew of B-17 and B-24 bombers, but he was never assigned to either plane. He finally made the crew of a B-29 bomber but never flew a combat mission. A good athlete in high school, Devine also played basketball at the Army Air Corps base in Springfield, Massachusetts—the birthplace of the sport.

When his military service was over, Devine attended the University of Minnesota–Duluth, where he served as captain of the basketball and football teams and was named the school's outstanding athlete as a senior in 1948.

Devine had to hitchhike part of the way to his first interview to become head football coach at East Jordan (Michigan) High School. After leading the high school to first-place finishes in two seasons, he left to serve as an assistant under Biggie Munn and Duffy Daugherty at Michigan State. Devine helped Michigan State defeat UCLA 28–20 in the 1953 Rose Bowl.

In 1955 Devine accepted the head coaching position at Arizona State, a school with a fledgling football program that was on probation for various violations. He arrived in Columbia after having guided the Sun Devils to a 27–3–1 record in three seasons.

"He was a wonderful coach," said All-America cornerback Roger Wehrli in *Tales from the Missouri Tigers*. "My two favorite coaches were Dan Devine and Don Coryell of the St. Louis Cardinals. They couldn't be two more opposites. Still, you had great respect for both of them. Coach Devine was a great motivator who got the most out of the players and the talent he had. He left

Beating Them Soundly

Dan Devine never met a team he couldn't beat. In fact, he defeated seventeen prominent college football programs more than 80 percent of the time (91-19-4). Here is Devine's record against those seventeen schools:

Alabama 3-0

Arkansas 1-0

Colorado 8-5

Florida 1-0

Illinois 3-0

Iowa State 11-1-1

Kansas 9-2-2

Kansas State 12-1

Miami (Fla.) 6-0

Michigan 4-1

Michigan State 5-1

Minnesota 3-0-1

Nebraska 8-5

Oklahoma State 10-1

Oregon 1-0

Purdue 5-1

Texas 1-0

most of the individual technique coaching up to the individual coaches. But he was a master at taking the team and getting it ready to play on Sunday."

Devine contributed to the University of Missouri as more than a football coach. He served as the school's athletic director from 1967 to 1970 and from 1992 to 1994.

In his first stint as athletic director, Devine made the decision to hire a young basketball coach from Northern Iowa, Norm Stewart. Stewart had been an All-America player at Missouri and went on to become one of the winningest basketball coaches in NCAA history. Devine also led the drive to build the Hearnes Center—a new fieldhouse and basketball arena named after then Missouri governor Warren Hearnes.

When Devine returned to Columbia as athletic director in the 1990s, attendance at football games had reached a thirty-three-year low. Devine restored pride in the school among Mizzou faithful—and also raised $2 million for improvements to the athletic facilities.

Devine's greatest talent, however, was coaching. When Duffy Daugherty became head football coach at Michigan State in 1954, he elevated Devine to his number-one assistant. One of Devine's main responsibilities was as lead recruiter.

"I guess he liked my personality," Devine wrote in his autobiography, *Simply Devine*, "or he thought I could get along well with the recruits, their families, and their high school coaches. Recruiting good players is, of course, the first requirement for building a successful program in any sport. It doesn't matter how great a coach is; if he doesn't have decent players on his team, he is not going to win."

Devine proved to be brilliant when it came to recruiting. As head coach at Arizona State, he lured Leon Burton, a star running back from Flint, Michigan, to Phoenix. Burton led the nation in yards per carry in 1957 and helped the Sun Devils to an undefeated record.

The great recruits kept coming at Missouri. The most notable Tigers Devine recruited include running back/defensive back Johnny Roland; cornerback Roger Wehrli; linebacker/running back Andy Russell; quarterbacks Gary Lane and Terry McMillan; running backs Charlie Brown, Jon Staggers, and Joe Moore; ends Conrad Hitchler, Bill Tobin, and Mel Gray; tackles Ed Blaine, Francis Peay, and Russ Washington; and guard Mike Carroll. Roland, Wehrli, Hitchler, Blaine, Peay, Washington, and Carroll eventually made All-America.

The recruitment of Russell, also an academic standout in high school who could have attended an Ivy League school, was a master stroke for Devine. According to Russell, Devine had the mayor of St. Louis and the governor of Missouri call his parents and enlisted big businessmen to tell Russell how bright his future would be if he went to MU. Russell also recalled that his parents went to Columbia without him, and that Devine sold his mother on the university by showing her the library.

"Dan Devine was a leader of men," said All-America defensive back Johnny Roland, one of the earliest African American recruits at the University of Missouri and a highly sought player from Corpus Christi, Texas, who spurned Oklahoma in favor of Missouri. "All the programs he undertook were better for it. He was my mentor. He recruited me to play at Missouri and he recruited me into the coaching profession. He had a way with people of making them believe in themselves."

After Devine got the recruits, he also knew how to motivate them to perform. Once, he kicked a player off the team for yawning, and legend has it that he once faked a heart attack to get his team's attention. The entire week before the 1969 Oklahoma game he played Oklahoma's fight song, "Boomer Sooner," so he could break the record in front of the team during a motivational speech on Friday. One detail Devine didn't account for was the fact that it was a vinyl record. When he tried to break it, all it did was bounce and bend. Finally, he threw it like a Frisbee in frustration.

"He was a great football coach on and off the field," said John Kadlec, an assistant for Devine. "He was a master at psyching up his players. He knew how to motivate them before a game and get their best efforts on the field. He did a great job of recruiting. In order to have championship teams, you have to have great players and a great coach."

Frank Broyles was the first Missouri coach to recruit African American players, bringing running backs Norris Stevenson and Mel West to Columbia in 1957. However, Devine, who took over for Broyles the following season, was the right person at the right time to guide the full racial integration of the Tigers football program.

When Devine arrived at Arizona State, it was the school's policy to segregate black and white players for sleeping and eating for road games. When he found out about the policy before a trip to play Hardin-Simmons in Abilene, Texas, Devine told the Arizona State athletic director that he didn't want to play a game under those conditions and asked him to eliminate the policy. The athletic director agreed.

"Our entire team walked into a nice hotel in Abilene, and only one person, an older gentleman dressed like a cowboy, raised his eyebrows as we walked through the lobby before he went back to reading his newspaper," said Devine in his autobiography. "My hard stance forced the school to change its policy, and I'm proud of that."

One of the first things Devine did at MU was to get a fraternity to stop flying a confederate flag and to have the band play "Fight Tiger" instead of "Dixie" as the fight song. Devine felt that both of those activities were offensive to black players and black students.

In Devine's first season at Missouri, the Tigers traveled to College Station, Texas, to play Texas A&M. When the team stopped to eat, the restaurant refused to serve the black players. Devine and the team decided to leave without eating. Missouri went on to lose the game 12–0.

"I broke down and cried, believing I had let my team down," said Devine in his autobiography. "I prided myself on preparation, every detail, and even though we had lost the game, having our players run into problems like this was far worse than losing a football game. I should have known this was a possibility and been prepared for it. I vowed to never again let something like this happen to my team."

Unfortunately, after the Tigers' victory over Navy in the 1960 Orange Bowl, Devine again was confronted by segregation. The airline that carried the team to Florida threw separate parties for blacks and whites after the game. Devine threw his own party and invited everyone.

Johnny Roland recalled another race-related incident during a trip to Kansas. The team stopped at a restaurant outside of

Kansas City, and the restaurant refused to serve black players. When Devine asked players what they wanted to do, they asked to leave without eating.

"I said I'll pay for the food because we've ordered it," Devine recalled to the *Kansas City Star* in 1995. "When I went up to pay for the food, I took a hundred-dollar bill out and threw it on the floor and rubbed it into some tobacco that was on the floor. Johnny almost grabbed me and said, 'Come on, Coach. It isn't worth it.'"

"He was colorblind," said Roland in *Tiger Tales*. "If you produced and performed for him on the football field, you were his guy. He was my mentor. He was the one who offered me a job. I took it and have been coaching ever since. In those days, I didn't think I would ever want to be a coach. He kept telling me, 'When you get done playing that silly little kid's game, I've got a job for you.'"

Devine wasn't just supportive of his players. During his term, Mizzou became the first Big Eight team to integrate its coaching staff with the hiring of Prentice Gautt in the mid-1960s.

It was in 1960 that Devine laid out four goals for his team. The first goal was to win the opening game of the year, which the Tigers had not done in the previous thirteen seasons. The second goal was to defeat Oklahoma at Norman, a feat the team had not accomplished since 1936. Third, the Tigers were going to win the conference championship, something they had not done since 1945. And fourth, they would win their first bowl game ever.

Using a modified version of the T formation and a powerful defense directed by new coordinator Al Onofrio, the Tigers didn't just win their opening game, they shut out a strong Southern

Methodist team 20–0 in front of 26,000 Missouri fans. The core group of fans grew dramatically as Missouri used a five-man blocking wedge to open holes on runs around the left and right ends.

Directing the Tigers' student body left and right plays was gritty quarterback Ron Taylor, who also was a devastating blocker. Mizzou gained 392 yards in a 28–7 victory over Oklahoma State in game two.

In week three Missouri helped christen Penn State's brand new Beaver Stadium. The Tigers spoiled the Nittany Lions' first game in the stadium by cruising to a 21–8 victory. Tiger end Danny LaRose gained national attention—which ultimately earned him All-America status—with a fierce pass rush that rattled Penn State quarterback Galen Hall. He also had a 16-yard touchdown reception for the Tigers' opening score.

Missouri traveled to Denver to face the Air Force Academy in week four and came away with an even more impressive 34–8 victory. The last time the Tigers had won their first four games was 1924.

From the Air Force game it was on to Manhattan, Kansas, to face former Tigers defensive coordinator Doug Weaver, who had become the head coach at Kansas State. The Tigers dispatched the Wildcats 45–0. The following week, in a 34–8 victory against Iowa State, Mizzou running back Donny Smith returned a punt 88 yards for a touchdown. The next week's 28–0 blasting of Nebraska was punctuated by a 69-yard touchdown run from Norris Stevenson.

Colorado scored first against the number-two-ranked Tigers, but a goal-line stand changed the momentum. Missouri's warm-up for Oklahoma was a tough test, but the Tigers managed a 16–6 victory.

Mizzou traveled to Norman with the nation's top-ranked rushing defense, allowing a meager 73 yards per game. And the Tigers had not surrendered a rushing touchdown in posting an 8–0 record.

But this was Oklahoma. In Missouri's past fourteen consecutive losses against Oklahoma, if things could go wrong, they usually did. And at first it seemed Missouri would be unable to break that pattern: On the first play from scrimmage, the Sooners ran a counter option and halfback Mike McClellan sprinted 70 yards for a touchdown.

But Mizzou refused to fold and, behind a 77-yard touchdown run from Stevenson and a 30-yard score by Smith, the Tigers led 24–12 at halftime. An Oklahoma touchdown cut the lead to 24–19, but LaRose made a huge tackle on a fourth-and-one play that stopped the Sooners late in the third quarter. On the first play of the fourth quarter, Stevenson broke free in front of the Oklahoma bench and ran 60 yards for a touchdown to put the game out of the Sooners' reach.

The overwhelming 41–19 victory put the state of Missouri into a frenzy. The Tigers jumped over the University of Minnesota for the first time in school history and were ranked number one in the nation by both the Associated Press and United Press International.

As the Tigers neared Columbia Regional Airport on the return flight from Norman, the plane had to circle a number of times because an estimated 20,000 people were all over the highways and runways. The police had to clear the runways, and fire trucks were at the airport to shuttle the team into Columbia.

It was standing-room-only at a rally at the student union.

1960: A Devine Season

9/17	Southern Methodist	20–0 W
9/24	Oklahoma State	28–7 W
10/1	at Penn State	21–8 W
10/8	Air Force at Denver	34–8 W
10/15	at Kansas State	45–0 W
10/22	Iowa State	34–8 W
10/29	at Nebraska	28–0 W
11/5	Colorado	16–6 W
11/12	at Oklahoma	41–19 W
11/19	Kansas	7–23 L*
1/2/1961	Orange Bowl vs. Navy	21–14 W

*Kansas later forfeited the game for using an ineligible player.

During the rally, Tigers player Rockne Calhoun told the Missouri faithful that he had always wanted to play for Mizzou and beat Oklahoma. "Today I did both, and now I can die," he said.

Legendary *St. Louis Post-Dispatch* columnist and editor Bob Broeg summed things up best in the lead of his game story: "The meek inherited the earth today. Mild-mannered Norris Stevenson, son of a St. Louis minister, ran 77 yards and 60 yards for touchdowns as unbeaten Missouri beat Oklahoma in Norman for the first time in 24 years."

Don Faurot (right) saw something special in Dan Devine, and Devine didn't let Mr. Missouri Football down.

The final game of the year was at home against a Kansas team that featured quarterback John Hadl and backs Curtis McClinton and Bert Coan. Distracted and tired, the Tigers lost 23–7 in a stunner. The Jayhawks held Missouri, which had averaged 280 rushing yards per game during their nine victories, to a meager 61 yards on the ground.

In the sixties the national champion was crowned before the bowl games. Minnesota was awarded the 1960 title after winning the Big Ten and matching the Tigers' 9–1 record.

Minnesota went on to lose to UCLA in the Rose Bowl. At the Orange Bowl, in front of President-elect and former Naval officer John F. Kennedy, Missouri defeated Navy and Heisman Trophy–winning running back Joe Bellino, 21–14.

Later the Jayhawks were forced to forfeit their victory over Missouri and the conference title when Coan was ruled to be ineligible. Ultimately, the Tigers officially posted a perfect record.

"Despite what the polls said, there was no doubt about who was the best team in the country," Devine said in his autobiography. "All of the Eastern media were covering the Orange Bowl and came away impressed with our players. That team was a national championship team and deserved to be recognized as such, and to this day my honest opinion is that I let it slip away from them. I can't go back and change it. That team bears a scar instead of a pat on the back, and it remains one of the biggest regrets of my life."

In 1971 Devine left Columbia for Green Bay, Wisconsin, to try his hand at coaching professional football's most storied franchise, the Green Bay Packers. Devine's best season was 1972, when he led the Packers to the NFC Central Division championship and was selected as the NFC coach of the year.

Devine lasted just four seasons in Green Bay, posting a 25–28–4 record. His most lasting accomplishment was bringing Bob Harlan from the St. Louis Cardinals to serve as an administrative assistant. Harlan, a graduate of Marquette University in Milwaukee, has been with the Packers ever since, eventually becoming the Packer organization's president and CEO. Harlan was greatly responsible for Green Bay's return to glory in the 1990s.

Early in his Missouri career, Devine was approached by Notre Dame to become its head coach. The timing wasn't right then, but it was in 1975. In six seasons he led the Fighting Irish to a 53–16–1 record, including a 3–1 mark in bowl games. In 1977 Devine—with the help of an unassuming quarterback named Joe Montana—guided the Irish to a 10–1 record. Their 38–10 victory over Texas in the Cotton Bowl earned Notre Dame a national championship.

Probably Devine's most memorable game was Notre Dame's 35–34 victory over Houston in the 1979 Cotton Bowl. In bitter cold, the Irish made a ferocious 20-point comeback in the second half, with Montana, who had been suffering from dehydration, leading the charge.

When Devine retired from coaching in 1980 because of his wife's health, he stood second behind Alabama's Paul "Bear" Bryant for the most victories in NCAA Division-I history, with an overall record of 127–41–7. And Devine had a 3–0 record head-to-head against the Bear.

No matter how many coaching stops Devine made along the way, his heart was always at Mizzou, which has won only 43 percent of its games since he left. Despite having won a national title at Notre Dame and having guided the NFL's winningest franchise, Devine wears a Missouri jacket and ring and holds a Tigers helmet on the cover of his autobiography.

Fear the Tiger

Onofrio Tries on Big Shoes

Replacing a coaching legend is extremely difficult. Football history, especially, is littered with those who have tried and didn't last.

The names that immediately come to mind include Phil Bengtson, who replaced Vince Lombardi of the Green Bay Packers; the Redskins' Richie Petitbon, who followed

Joe Gibbs; and Hunk Anderson, Luke Johnsos, Paddy Driscoll, and Jim Dooley, all of whom tried at different times to fill the shoes of Chicago Bears legend George Halas.

In the college ranks there are Gomer Jones and Gary Gibbs, who had to live in the shadows of Bud Wilkinson and Barry Switzer, respectively. Ray Perkins took over for Paul "Bear" Bryant at Alabama. Before going to the Bears, Hunk Anderson lasted three seasons following Knute Rockne, and Bob Davie struggled after Lou Holtz at Notre Dame.

Al Onofrio never gave much thought to becoming a head coach. Lured from coaching golf to coaching on the gridiron by head coach Dan Devine when the two were at Arizona State University in the early 1950s, Onofrio played the role of wise confidant and stabilizing influence for the fiery young Devine.

When Devine became head football coach at the University of Missouri in 1958, he asked Onofrio to join him. As defensive coordinator during Mizzou's most illustrious decade, Onofrio was a master at putting together game plans that stymied opponents.

When Devine decided to take the head coaching position with the Green Bay Packers after the 1970 college season, he again summoned Onofrio. This time, however, Missouri also wanted the coach, who was a fan and player favorite.

"He was a classic and classy gentleman," said former Tigers quarterback Pete Woods (1974 to 1977) following Onofrio's death in 2004. "For a lot of us, he was a real father figure. He was not just a coach we respected, but a man we looked up to in a lot of ways."

Onofrio became the Tigers' head coach in 1971 and promptly went 1–10. In a roller-coaster pattern that marked his seven years as head coach, Onofrio helped Mizzou rebound with a 6–5 record and an invitation to the Fiesta Bowl in 1972. The Associated Press selected him as the Big Eight Coach of the Year.

The 1972 campaign began on the upswing as the Tigers unexpectedly defeated Oregon and star quarterback Dan Fouts 24–22 in Columbia. However, the next four games produced wild swings—a demoralizing 27–0 loss to Baylor, a 34–27 victory over California, a 17–16 defeat to Oklahoma State, and a 62–0 blanking by Nebraska—the worst defeat for Missouri since a 65–0 loss to Texas in 1932.

Next on Missouri's schedule was a trip to South Bend, Indiana, to face the unbeaten and eighth-ranked Fighting Irish of Notre Dame. By this time the Tigers had done little to suggest that they were any better than the overwhelming underdog tag they had acquired.

In a constant light rain, Missouri was nearly flawless in a 30–26 victory over Notre Dame. Tigers running backs Don Johnson (87 rushing yards and 2 touchdowns) and Junior College All-American Tommy Reamon (73 yards) paced a ball-control ground attack that accounted for 72 of Mizzou's 79 offensive plays. Greg Hill added 3 field goals, and John Cherry completed 4 of 5 passes for 106 yards. The Tigers did not commit a turnover; the Fighting Irish lost 2 fumbles and threw 2 interceptions.

After Mizzou's stunning performance, legendary Nebraska coach Bob Devaney sent Onofrio a letter that said, "I sincerely believe that your preparation—mentally, physically, and technically—was the best job done by any coach in the history of football."

Onofrio had won just three of his first sixteen games; however, the Notre Dame victory was the turning point that put the bite back into the Tigers' program. Despite finishing with a

38–41 career record, Onofrio proved to be the master of the upset. Teams shuddered at the prospect of facing a hungry and resilient Missouri team.

The week following Notre Dame, Mizzou got a game-winning field goal from Hill with 59 seconds remaining for a 20–17 victory over seventh-ranked Colorado. Another game-winning field goal by Hill, with 1:27 remaining, gave Missouri a 6–5 victory over twelfth-ranked Iowa State and a final regular-season record of 6–5.

Over the next five seasons, Onofrio's Tigers would upset number-two-ranked Nebraska (1973), seventh-ranked Arizona State (1974), twelfth-ranked Nebraska (1974), and second-ranked Ohio State (1976). In 1975 a 20–7 victory in a nationally televised Monday night game against second-ranked Alabama elicited the following comment from Crimson Tide head coach Bear Bryant: "You kicked the hell out of us. You should have scored 40."

In 1976 the Tigers spoiled the debut of USC's coach John Robinson by knocking off the eighth-ranked Trojans 46–25 in Los Angeles. USC did not lose another game that season.

According to Onofrio, he learned from Devine to sacrifice everything for a team that was ready emotionally and physically to play hard at every snap. Precision and effort in blocking, tackling, and pursuing were more important than mere athletic ability. Onofrio's ideals were echoed by his former players, including South Florida head coach Jim Leavitt, who played defensive back for Onofrio and the Tigers from 1974 to 1977.

"He always said to play with reckless abandon," Leavitt said. "I'll never forget that. He was my coach, he was the one who

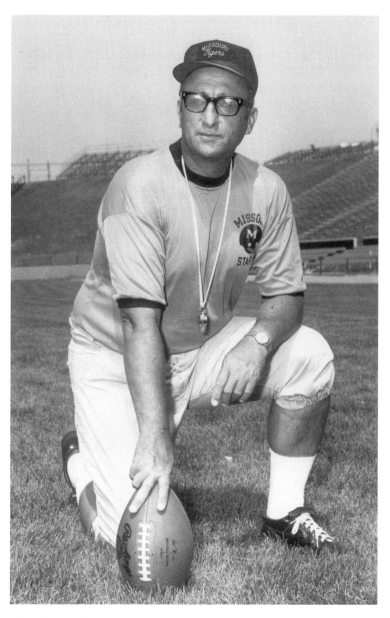

Al Onofrio knew how to win big games. However, he couldn't find a way to get past Kansas.

recruited me to Missouri, and his career as a head coach was basically my career there."

Onofrio produced a sterling 18–10 record against some of the biggest names in college football. In 1973 the Tigers finished 8–4 and ranked seventeenth in the nation. Mizzou defeated Auburn 34–17 in the Sun Bowl.

Ironically, Onofrio's biggest contributions to the Tigers' incredible run during the 1960s—a strong defense and consistency—were the very things that eluded him as a head coach. From 1960 to 1969 Missouri allowed a total of 944 points. In Onofrio's seven years as head coach, the Tigers surrendered nearly twice as many points (1,536). Against Big Eight opponents, Onofrio was a woeful 20–31.

Ultimately, his inability to defeat archrival Kansas proved to be Onofrio's undoing. By 1977 the Tigers were an extremely unacceptable 1–6 against the Jayhawks, and three of those losses came when Mizzou was ranked.

"I always told him he was so good as a coach that he could have tripped on his beard if he had just beaten Kansas," said former *St. Louis Post-Dispatch* sports editor and columnist Bob Broeg. "He was favored five of the seven times he played them and lost six of seven. It was diabolical."

"I thought for the most part we were the better team in those years," Jim Leavitt said. "We had beaten Alabama, Southern Cal, Ohio State, Nebraska twice. But we only beat Kansas once. I felt like in some of those games, it made their season to beat us."

Onofrio never coached again after his Missouri days. However, he stayed very close to the university, maintaining contact with players and making numerous public appearances.

"Everyone associated with Missouri should be thankful for the time he spent here and how much he meant to the institution by what he brought not only with his football expertise, but also his character," said Missouri athletic director Mike Alden following Onofrio's death.

Shucking the Huskers

To say that the Nebraska-Missouri rivalry started off on the wrong foot for the Tigers in the 1970s would be a gross understatement. Missouri began the decade by losing its first three meetings with the Cornhuskers by a combined score of 119–7.

In 1973 Nebraska, the second-ranked team in the country, was poised to increase its scoring margin against the surprising twelfth-ranked Tigers, who had won their first four games. A record crowd of 68,170 at Memorial Stadium in Columbia was cautiously optimistic that Mizzou at least would be able to improve on its 62–0 pounding at the hands of Nebraska the previous year.

Missouri's faithful fans got their first wish with a low-scoring affair. Using a defense reminiscent of Tigers head coach Al Onofrio's stingy units from the 1960s, when he was the team's defensive coordinator, Mizzou limited Nebraska to two field goals in its first three series.

The Cornhuskers were chewing up yardage (they would finish the game with a 444–170 advantage in total yards), but the Tigers produced boosts of momentum with timely big plays.

Leading 6–0, Nebraska safety Randy Borg intercepted Tigers quarterback John Cherry and returned the ball to the Tigers' 35 yard line. The Cornhuskers gained 6 yards on their next three plays and then decided to go for it on fourth-and-four at Missouri's 29. Nebraska quarterback David Humm dropped back to pass but was sacked by Tiger defensive lineman Herris Butler.

Mizzou answered with a twelve-play drive that ended with a 35-yard field goal by Greg Hill. With 1:04 remaining in the half, Humm fumbled a handoff exchange and Butler was there again for the recovery. Three plays later, Hill kicked a 31-yard field goal to tie the game at 6–6.

Midway through the third quarter, Butler blocked a Nebraska field goal attempt. With a little more than four minutes remaining in the game, the Tigers' diminutive defensive back John Moseley intercepted Humm's pass and returned the ball to midfield.

Mizzou was forced to punt on the ensuing series, but Borg fumbled. All-America center Scott Anderson fell on the ball at Nebraska's 4 yard line with 2:35 remaining.

"I snapped the ball and nobody held me," Anderson told reporters after the game. "I went down the field and nobody touched me. The guy caught the ball, and then he juggled it and went to his knees. The ball was just there. I went for it and was fortunate enough to get it. It's a great thrill for a lineman."

With 2:01 to go, fullback Tom Mulkey scored the first Tigers touchdown against the Cornhuskers in three seasons on a 1-yard run up the middle to give Missouri a 13–6 lead. Nebraska wasn't done, though. Humm led his school on a four-play, 72-yard drive that culminated with a 22-yard scoring pass to Rich Bahe.

If you've ever wondered why Nebraska head coach Tom Osborne decided to go for 2 points and a win rather than kick an

Highlights from the Days of Disco

The 1970s produced a host of memorable games and individual performances. Following are just a few of the individual bests from a rock-and-roll
decade:

When Mizzou trailed Arizona State 28–7 at halftime of the 1972 Fiesta
Bowl, Mike Fink returned a kickoff 100 yards for a school-record touchdown and running back Tommy Reamon rushed for 155 yards to get the
Tigers back into the game. Ultimately the Sun Devils, who amassed 718
yards of total offense, won the shootout 49–35.

All-America defensive back John Moseley averaged a school-record
13.3 yards per kickoff return from 1971 to 1973.

Running back Tony Galbreath rushed for 130 yards in a 21–10 victory
over Nebraska at Lincoln in 1974.

Galbreath, who would go on to an twelve-year NFL career with the
Saints, Vikings, and Giants, had 120 rushing yards in a 20–7 victory on
national television over second-ranked Alabama in 1975.

Wide receiver Henry Marshall earned All-America honors in 1975 after
catching 44 passes for 945 yards and 9 touchdowns.

Quarterback Steve Pisarkiewicz set a school record with 371 passing
yards in a 41–14 victory over fourteenth-ranked Oklahoma State in 1975.

Jeff Brockhaus's 33-yard field goal provided the only points in Missouri's 3–0 upset of Notre Dame in 1978.

Quarterback Phil Bradley had a 69-yard touchdown run and Russ Calabrese returned an interception 30 yards for a score in a 38–20 loss to
number-two Alabama in 1978.

The Tigers set a variety of records in their 45–15 victory over San
Diego State in 1979. Mizzou came from behind by scoring all 45 points
after intermission, a school mark for most points in half. Thirty-one of
those points came in the fourth quarter, an all-time school record for a
quarter. Cornerback Eric Wright, who eventually would earn four Super
Bowl rings with the 49ers, intercepted a Tigers' single-game-record 3
passes against San Diego State. Bill Whitaker, a 1980 All-American,
matched Wright's interception mark in the same game.

In 1979 running back Gerry Ellis rushed for 173 yards in a 14–6 victory over Illinois.

extra point for a tie for the national championship in the 1983 Orange Bowl against the Miami Hurricanes, look no further than the 1973 game against the Missouri Tigers—in Osborne's debut season as the Cornhuskers' head coach.

Rather than settle for a tie with Mizzou, Osborne decided to go for 2. Humm rolled to his left on the conversion attempt, but Tigers lineman Bob McRoberts tipped the pass and Tony Gillick intercepted it to cement an amazing 13–12 victory.

"Missouri had lots going psychologically, and they played a very emotional game," said Osborne. "We just couldn't overcome the mistakes we made."

Nebraska spent the rest of the decade struggling to overcome Missouri, which won four of its next seven meetings with the Cornhuskers. All four of those victories came with Nebraska nationally ranked—second (1973), twelfth (1974), third (1976), and second (1978).

Running back Tony Galbreath, a native of Fulton, Missouri, and sophomore quarterback Steve Pisarkiewicz, who hailed from St. Louis, led the Tigers to a 21–10 victory over Nebraska with more than 75,000 Cornhusker fans looking on at Lincoln in 1974. In 1976 the Tigers defeated eighth-ranked USC in Los Angeles and second-ranked Ohio State in Columbus, before traveling to Lincoln to face the third-ranked Cornhuskers.

Mizzou showed the same respect to Nebraska that it had to the Trojans and Buckeyes. A school-record 98-yard touchdown pass from quarterback Pete Woods to Joe Stewart keyed a 34–24 upset. Stewart caught three passes for 145 yards, averaging a school single-game record 48.3 yards per reception. Future Pro Football Hall of Fame and All-America tight end Kellen Winslow scored his first touchdown for the Tigers on a 9-yard catch from Woods.

The Tigers had nothing to lose when they returned to Lincoln in 1978. With a 6–4 record, 13-point underdog Mizzou was facing the nation's second-ranked team, a squad that was headed to the Orange Bowl to play for a possible national title.

On Nebraska's first play from scrimmage, running back Rick Berns raced 82 yards around end for a touchdown and a 7–0 score. Berns finished the game with a Nebraska-record 255 rushing yards, but Missouri was able to weather the storm.

Running back James Wilder, who hailed from Sikeston, Missouri, countered Berns, rushing for 181 yards and tying a school record with 4 rushing touchdowns in a 35–31 victory. Winslow caught nine passes for 132 yards, including a 14-yard touchdown reception from Phil Bradley. The Tigers finished with 476 total yards of offense to Nebraska's 517 in the seesaw battle.

"Nebraska was number two and going to the Orange Bowl," said Missouri defensive end Wendell Ray in 1978. "And we beat them. We were just the better football team."

Phil Was Phil Before Bo Knew Bo

It's not often in college sports that you get a two-for-one with players. Before there was Bo Jackson, there was Missouri's Phil Bradley, who dominated on the football and baseball fields.

"I was looking to go play two sports somewhere," said Bradley in *Tiger Tales*. "I knew the history of Missouri, that they played competitive schedules and were a successful program. I think I was recruited as a football player who had intentions of playing

Phil Bradley was a football star at Missouri, but he made his professional fortunes as an outfielder in Major League Baseball.

baseball. We had three winning seasons out of four and played in three bowl games. I had the opportunity to play with a lot of good football players. When I left in 1980, I was the all-time total offense leader in the Big Eight Conference."

A starter from the second game of his freshman season, Bradley dazzled Missouri fans with his strong arm and quick feet. From 1977 to 1980 he guided the Tigers to twenty-seven victories, led the team in total yardage each year, and was selected as the Big Eight Conference Player of the Year three times.

Bradley also rose to the occasion in bowl games, leading Mizzou to a 20–15 victory over LSU in the 1978 Liberty Bowl and a 24–14 defeat of South Carolina and future Heisman Trophy–winning running back George Rogers in the 1979 Hall of Fame Bowl. His 210 passing yards in a 28–25 loss to Purdue in the 1980 Liberty Bowl still rank as the most in a bowl game by a Tigers quarterback.

Bradley passed for a career-high 295 yards against Oklahoma State in 1978, and he ranks third in Missouri history with ten games of 200 or more passing yards. He is second on the school's all-time list in passing yards (5,352), total yards (6,459), and touchdown passes (32).

Bradley had a brilliant college football career, but he was an even better baseball player. The first—and only—University of Missouri baseball player to have his number (15) retired, he had a career .362 batting average for the Tigers, including an incredible 1981 season in which he hit .457, scored 77 runs, had 40 RBI, and was selected All-America. Snubbed by both the NFL and CFL, Bradley signed with Major League Baseball's Seattle Mariners after being selected in the third round in 1981. In 1983

Powering Forward

Kansas City native Warren Powers posted a 46–33–3 record (.580 winning percentage) in seven seasons (1978 to 1984) as head football coach at the University of Missouri. Here are a few highlights from the career of the third-winningest coach in school history:

- Named team MVP as a senior defensive back at the University of Nebraska in 1962.

- Played defensive back with the Oakland Raiders from 1963 to 1968, leading the team in interceptions in 1965 and 1966 and starting at strong safety in Super Bowl II.

- Became head coach at Missouri after one season at Washington State University (and had to pay $55,000 to get out of his contract with the Cougars).

- Won his first three games against Kansas and earned bowl berths in each of those seasons.

- Had a 3–2 overall record in bowl games, winning the Liberty Bowl (1978), Hall of Fame Bowl (1979), and Tangerine Bowl (1981).

- Faced the number-one (Notre Dame) and number-two (Alabama) nationally ranked teams in the first two games of his debut season at Missouri. The Tigers defeated the top-ranked Fighting Irish, coached by Mizzou legend Dan Devine and quarterbacked by Joe Montana, 3–0. They lost 38–20 to the Crimson Tide.

- Was selected as the Walter Camp Coach of the Year following the 1978 season.

- Led Missouri to a 19–14 victory over fifteenth-ranked Oklahoma in 1981.

he made the Mariners' major-league roster and played five seasons for the club, earning All-Star honors in 1985. During his eight-year career, Bradley, who also played with Philadelphia (1988), Baltimore (1989 and 1990), and the Chicago White Sox (1990), batted .286, hit 78 home runs, and stole 155 bases.

Bradley was so good a left fielder that the Mariners still were looking for his replacement more than fifteen years after he last played for Seattle. "It's been a long time since the Phil Bradley days, when we had a legitimate left fielder who could pretty much do it all and play every day," said Mariners outfield coach Johnny Moses in 2003.

Bradley could do it all for the Mariners. And he did it all for Ol' Mizzou.

Roller-coaster Ride

From the mid-1980s through the 1990s, Tiger football fell far short of expectations for the Missouri faithful. Woody's Wagon broke down; Air Stull crashed; and Larry Smith couldn't win the big games. Throughout those fifteen years, Mizzou took a roller-coaster ride marked by near misses and sterling individual performances.

The up-and-down nature of the 1980s and 1990s is epitomized by the fact that three of the four greatest single-game turnarounds happened during these two decades. In 1986 Missouri followed a 77–0 loss to Oklahoma with a 48–0 trouncing of Kansas for an incredible 125-point swing, the greatest ever. Third on the list was a 51–21 defeat of Kansas State after a 55–0 loss to Miami—a difference of 86 points. And in 1990 Missouri experienced a 72-point swing when it lost 58–7 at home to Indiana and came back with a 30–9 victory over twenty-first-ranked Arizona State.

Woody Widenhofer, who helped the Pittsburgh Steelers win four Super Bowls as an assistant coach, was a brilliant recruiter who lured St. Louis prep stars, such as running back and *Parade Magazine* High School Player of the Year Tony VanZant and All-America quarterback Ronnie Cameron, and out-of-state headliners, such as defensive end Jeff Cross from California and cornerback Adrian Jones from Dania, Florida. However, the best record Woody's recruits could muster was a 5–6 finish in 1987. Missouri opened that season 4–2 but lost four of five down the stretch.

Bob Stull brought to Columbia the most prolific passing offense that Missouri has ever seen. Quarterback Jeff Handy, who played from 1991 to 1994, set school records for passing attempts and completions in a game (73 and 43, respectively, against Oklahoma State in 1992), season (349 and 200 in 1994), and career (1,058 and 618).

Handy also set Tigers' marks for passing yards in a game (480 against Oklahoma State in 1992), season (2,436 in 1992), and career (6,959). His 39 career touchdown passes are an all-time Missouri record. In 1990 Handy's predecessor, Kent Kiefer, set a school record by passing for more than 200 yards in eight games.

Quarterback Jeff Handy was an offensive force, but his impressive passing statistics didn't produce many victories.

Stull's wide-open game plans made games exciting for fans, but unfortunately they didn't translate into victories. He had a tough first season (1989), losing to number-two-ranked Miami, third-ranked Colorado, and fourth-ranked Nebraska by a combined score of 137–17, and things never got much better. During his five-year stint at the Tigers' helm, Stull never led the team to more than four victories in a season.

"In coaching, you're either way up or way down—there's hardly anything that's in between," Stull said in 1998. "If you win, you win and you're fired up. If you lose, you're sick to your stomach. And even if you win, it's not so much celebration as it's just relief."

Larry Smith led the Tigers to their first two winning seasons since 1984 and final rankings of twenty-third and twenty-first in the nation in 1997 and 1998. In '98 Missouri set a school record for scoring with 368 points and was nationally ranked every week of the regular season except week one. But Smith couldn't defeat the nation's elite. He posted a combined record of 1–20 against opponents ranked in the Associated Press's top twenty-five.

Despite a dearth of victories, not everything was disappointing during the 1980s and 1990s. Some of the most productive players in Missouri history starred during that time.

The Tigers' running game was especially potent. Running back Devin West (1995 to 1998) finished his career as the Tigers' all-time leader in all-purpose yards with 3,824 (2,954 rushing, 219 receiving, and 654 return). He is followed by Brock Olivo (1994 to 1997) with 3,475 and Darrell Wallace (1984 to 1987) with 3,303.

Wide receiver Kenny Holly (1990 to 1993) set a school record with 151 career receptions. Another receiver, Victor Bailey, caught a single-season record 75 passes in 1992.

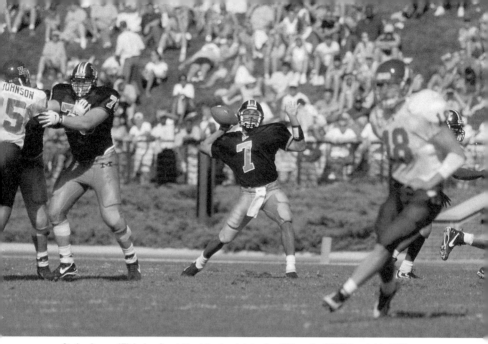

Corby Jones (7) helped put the bite back into the Tigers. In 1997 he guided Mizzou to its first winning season in fourteen years.

Jeff Jacke (1988 to 1992) left Missouri as the school's all-time scoring leader among kickers with 225 points. His 5-field-goal, 1-extra-point, 16-total-point performance against Kansas in 1992 still stands as a single-game scoring mark among college kickers. Tom Whelihan, who kicked for Mizzou from 1984 to 1987, was an All-America candidate and finished as the Tigers' all-time leader with 44 field goals.

There were more than enough reasons to keep Missouri fans filling Faurot Field on Saturdays during the 1980s and 1990s. And the love of everything Ol' Mizzou was at the top of the list.

Don Faurot always said that "Missoura" boys were more than good enough to put the Tigers in the national spotlight. And it was two homegrown players who helped bring Mizzou out of one of the darkest football eras in school history.

Corby Jones was a highly recruited quarterback from Columbia's Hickman High School who grew up immersed in Missouri football. Running back Devin West went to Moberly High School just thirty miles north of Columbia along Highway 63 and was a work in progress when he arrived at Mizzou. Roommates since their freshman years in 1995, Jones and West took different routes to stardom. But their combined success has a special place in Missouri lore.

Curtis Jones, who was the eleventh of thirteen children and grew up in poverty in St. Louis, played two seasons as a nose tackle for the Tigers in the late sixties and three years (1968 to 1970) as a linebacker in the NFL. When his playing days were finished, he embarked on a coaching career and served as a Tigers assistant in the 1970s. When Curtis returned to Missouri as an assistant in 1993, he was ready to give the rest of his life to the school that had given him so much.

When Curtis's son Corby told Curtis that he had decided to attend Mizzou instead of Nebraska or Illinois, all Curtis could say was, "Thank you."

It didn't take long for Missouri fans to thank both Curtis and Corby. Following a 30–0 loss to Kansas State that produced only 118 yards on offense in the fifth game of the 1995 college season, Tigers head coach Larry Smith made a bold decision.

"He [Smith] said, 'We want you to play,'" said Corby, who was supposed to redshirt as a freshman. "My eyes were watering up. I said, 'Thank you. Thank you for the opportunity. I'll be ready to go.'"

Corby's first start came against Nebraska in Lincoln, and to say it didn't go well would be an understatement. The 6-foot 1-

Rushing into History

Five of the top six rushers in Missouri history played during the 1980s and 1990s.

Zach Abron	2000–03	3,198 yards
Brock Olivo	1994–97	3,026 yards
Devin West	1995–98	2,954 yards
Darrell Wallace	1984–87	2,607 yards
Corby Jones	1995–98	2,533 yards

Zach Abron

inch, 222-pound athlete attempted only two passes, completing one to a Cornhusker defender. Jones ran eight times for 7 yards in a 57–0 loss.

Things definitely got better for Jones, though. In 1997 he led the Tigers to their first winning season since 1983 and finished his Missouri career by guiding the team to victory in thirteen of his final seventeen games, including a 34–31 win over West Virginia in the 1999 Insight.com Bowl.

Jones said near the end of his senior year that he wanted to be remembered as someone who went out and played every game like it was the last game he would ever play. "I went out and played with emotion, heart, and a lot of pride in the program," he said.

Jones's name appears throughout the Tigers' record books. He ranks second on the school's all-time scoring list, with 228 points and 38 rushing touchdowns.

In 1997 against Oklahoma State, Jones tied Terry McMillan's Mizzou record by producing 6 touchdowns (2 rushing and 4 passing). Against Iowa State the same season, he posted the highest single-game passer rating (270.7) in school history. Jones set a record for total offense in a season with 2,545 (887 rushing, 1,658 passing) in 1997, and he is the Tigers' all-time touchdown leader with 84.

Before Jones's brilliant senior year in 1998, his father, Curtis, died of a heart attack at age fifty-five. Despite the personal tragedy, Corby led the Tigers to a twenty-first ranking in the final national polls.

"Corby Jones was one of the greatest athletes to ever play at Mizzou," said John Kadlec, who has been associated with the

Tigers since the 1940s as a player, coach, and broadcaster. "He had a knack for football. He could run and throw equally well. As a quarterback, he knew when to run. He had great instincts, which is what separates great players from good ones. His judgment was impeccable."

Devin West's father abandoned his family when Devin was eight. Eventually, Devin's mother moved him and two brothers from Kansas City to Moberly for a quieter life. West was student manager for the Moberly High School football team until a friend persuaded him to play.

West played well enough to earn a scholarship at Missouri. However, unlike Jones, West sat on the bench as a freshman and sophomore.

"I was the patient one," West said. "I waited my turn. When I got my chance I did everything I could to help our team, to help us be the best we could be."

Devin West made the most of his opportunities. In his only season as the featured back, in 1998, he tied legendary Tigers back Bob Steuber for the most touchdowns (18) and also set school records for carries (283) and rushing yards (1,578) in a season.

West finished his Missouri career as the all-time leader with 3,824 combined yards (2,954 rushing, 219 receiving, and 654 returning). He is third behind Zach Abron (252 points) and Corby Jones with 174 career points, and his 2,954 rushing yards put him third behind Abron and Brock Olivo.

"Devin was a powerful runner with a nose for finding holes," Kadlec said. "It's amazing to know that he went from being a student manager in high school to a college star. And don't forget both Jones and West had a great offensive line."

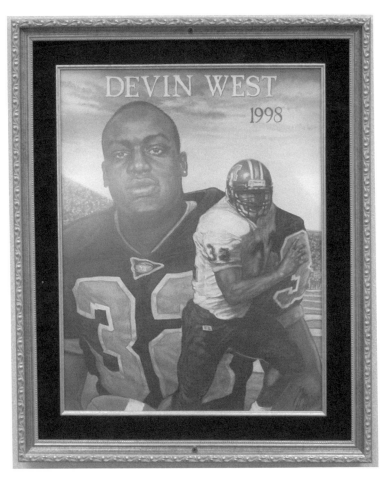

Devin West finished his college career as Missouri's all-time leader with 3,824 total yards (2,954 rushing, 219 receiving, and 654 returning).

Roommates since their freshman seasons, Corby and Devin became more like family than friends. They cried and grieved together when Corby learned about his dad's death.

"We're just like brothers," Jones said in 1998. "I don't know who's the older brother and who's the younger brother, that kind of varies. But it means a lot, having him around. It's great to have somebody that close to me."

"Brothers are forever," West said. "He's going to always be my brother, no matter where he goes or no matter where I go. I'm still going to call him up, talk to him, come out and see him."

"When you see kids bond like that, it's part of the college experience," Smith said. "They make friendships and relationships that last the rest of their lives. . . . That's what we try to stress with our program, that we're a family."

Another member of the Mizzou family was Bill McCartney. He played for Missouri from 1959 to 1961. However, Mizzou fans remember McCartney more for what he did *to* the Tigers than what he did *for* the Tigers.

October 6, 1990, is a day that will live in infamy for anyone who calls Ol' Mizzou home. On that day, what should have been one of the greatest victories in school history inexplicably turned into one of Missouri's most bitter defeats.

The Tigers were coming off an impressive 30–9 victory over twenty-first-ranked Arizona State when McCartney returned to Columbia as head football coach at the University of Colorado. McCartney's Buffaloes were ranked twelfth nationally, and the coach had visions of a repeat Big Eight Conference championship, maybe even a national title.

Although the Tigers were massive underdogs to Colorado, the game was a seesaw battle, and Missouri had a 31–27 lead with close to a minute left in the game.

The Buffaloes frantically drove down the field and moved the ball to Mizzou's 3 yard line with 31 seconds left in the game. What followed is college football history.

Pro Tigers

Ranging from tight end Kellen Winslow, who is the only Tigers football player inducted into the Pro Football Hall of Fame, to running back Bill Ziegler, who had a cup of coffee with the Calgary Stampeders of the Canadian Football League, the University of Missouri football program has seen 189 of its lettermen join the professional ranks.

The 1980s may well have been a lost decade for Missouri football, but those years were not without stars, producing the most professional football players (53) of any decade in school history. Leading the charge for the Tigers in the eighties were cornerback Otis Smith, who won a Super Bowl ring as a starter for the New England Patriots in 2001 and shares an NFL record with two interceptions returned for a touchdown in a game; safety Erik McMillan, who played in two Pro Bowls (1989 and 1990) while with the Jets and is the son of NFL great Ernie McMillan; and defensive end Jeff Cross, a 1991 Pro Bowl selection while with the Dolphins.

Other decades produced the following number of professionals: 2000s (6), 1990s (22), 1970s (45), 1960s (38), 1950s (16), 1940s (12), and 1930s and 1920s (5). The first Missouri players to compete professionally were all tackles— Ed "Brick" Travis (1921 Rock Island, 1923 St. Louis), Charles Van Dyne (1925 Buffalo), and Herbert Blumer (1925–1933 Chicago Cardinals).

Colorado had only one time out left when the Buffaloes completed the play that gave them first-and-goal at the 3, so quarterback Charles Johnson spiked the ball to stop the clock. On second down, running back Eric Bieniemy pounded up the middle for a yard, forcing Colorado to use its final time out. With 18 seconds remaining, the Buffaloes should have been facing third down. However, the officials failed to tell the chain gang to change the down marker from second to third down. Bieniemy tried to leap over the top on the next play, but Mizzou's Tom Reiner, Mike Riggenberg, and Maurice Benson were there to stop him.

The officials stopped the clock momentarily with 8 seconds remaining, and Johnson quickly spiked the ball to stop it again. The game should have ended with a Missouri celebration, but the down marker said fourth down. Johnson ran the ball into the end zone over the right side on the next down (down number five).

Angry fans stormed the field. A police officer and a female spectator were taken to the hospital with minor injuries suffered during the stampede. A cameraman fought with a ball boy who was wearing a Big Eight Conference T-shirt. Officials argued with reporters.

Only once before in NCAA history had this happened. Undefeated Cornell scored a game-winning touchdown on a fifth down against Dartmouth in 1940. Cornell subsequently refused the victory when they found out about the mistake.

Colorado and McCartney were not as magnanimous. Big Eight Conference administrators said there was nothing that could be done to reverse the final outcome—a 33–31 victory by the Buffaloes.

McCartney was defiant after the game and ranted about the

Mizzou's All-Century Football Team

In October 1990 more than 4,000 people voted for a twenty-five-member All-Century Football Team at Mizzou. The team was introduced at the 1990 Homecoming game against Kansas State.

Quarterbacks

Paul Christman	1938–1940
Phil Bradley	1977–1980
Terry McMillan	1968–69
Anton Stankowski	1915–19

Running Backs

Bob Steuber	1940–42
Harry Ice	1940–41
Joe Moore	1968–1970
Tony Galbreath	1974
James Wilder	1978–1980

Receivers

Kellen Winslow	1976–78
Mel Gray	1968–1970
Henry Marshall	1972–75
Leo Lewis III	1975–78

Linemen

Ed "Brick" Travis	1919–1920
Darold Jenkins	1940–41
Francis Peay	1964–65
Russ Washington	1965–67
Brad Edelman	1978–1981

Linebackers

Andy Russell	1960–62
Gus Otto	1962–64
Van Darkow	1979–81

Defensive Backs

Roger Wehrli	1966–68
Johnny Roland	1962–65
Eric Wright	1978–1980
Erik McMillan	1984–87

Coach

Dan Devine	1958–1970

soggy conditions of Faurot Field. (By his account, Buffaloes players slipped more than ninety times during the game.) McCartney later said he would not have complained about the field if he had known about the extra down.

"If I were a Missouri fan, and I felt like I had been cheated, and then here's this guy complaining about something else, I can understand the anger," McCartney, a devout Christian, told the *St. Louis Post-Dispatch*. "It's real important that I tell you this, because a lot of people have attacked my integrity on the sportsmanship issue. There's a verse in the scriptures that expresses how I feel better that anything I could say. What it [I Corinthians 4:4] says is my conscience is clear, but that does not make me innocent. It is the Lord who judges me. That's how I really feel, and that's really why even though I know a lot of people are mad and will be forever—people that I know even—that's why I don't fret over it too much."

After going on to defeat Notre Dame in the Orange Bowl, the 11–1–1 Buffaloes were awarded a share of the 1990 national championship with Georgia Tech. In Missouri, everyone knows that Colorado really finished 10–2–1.

The Renaissance

It's not often that a loss marks the revival of a football program. However, that's exactly what happened on November 8, 1997, at Memorial Stadium in Columbia, when top-ranked Nebraska defeated Missouri 45–38 in overtime.

The narrow loss by the 29-point underdog Tigers propelled them into the Associated Press top-twenty-five rankings (at number twenty-five) for the first time since 1983. The game also served notice to bowl committees around the country that Mizzou was back.

Despite the national attention, the "moral" victory was difficult to accept by the sellout crowd of 66,846 and by Tigers' faithful watching the game around the country. With 4:39 remaining in the game, quarterback Corby Jones threw a 15-yard touchdown pass to Eddie Brooks to give Missouri a 38–31 lead and seemingly an end to a losing streak against the Cornhuskers that dated to 1978.

On the ensuing series, the Tigers limited the Cornhuskers to only 5 yards on three plays, forcing a Nebraska punt. Missouri then used a six-play drive to take more precious time off the clock.

However, Nebraska got the ball back on its own 33 yard line with 55 seconds remaining. In eleven plays, the Cornhuskers moved the ball to the Tigers' 12 yard line. Then—on third-and-10 with 7 seconds remaining—it happened.

The Cornhuskers called "Shotgun 99 Double Slant," and quarterback Scott Frost dropped back to pass, looking for receiver Lance Brown. Brown was covered, so Frost moved to his second option and fired a bullet toward Shevin Wiggins, who had two Tigers prowling around him.

Missouri free safety Julian Jones stripped the ball from Wiggins's hands, but just before the ball hit the turf, Wiggins inexplicably kicked it over his head and toward the end zone, where Matt Davison was standing. Davison scooped up the ball into his arms.

Releasing nineteen years of pent-up frustration, Missouri fans stormed the north end zone, believing that the pass was incomplete and victory was theirs. Unfortunately, officials ruled the Immaculate Reception II a touchdown, and Kris Brown's extra point sent the game into overtime. Nebraska won on a 10-yard touchdown run by Frost. It was the first overtime game in the Cornhuskers' history.

"I saw the ball get deflected off Shevin," Davison said. "It was floating like a punt, kind of end over end. It just seemed like it took forever to get there. It was probably a few inches off the ground when I caught it. I was just hoping the refs were going to call it a catch."

"He never had it—it hit the ground and then he scooped it back up," Tigers linebacker Al Sterling said. "I was standing right there. That was not a touchdown. In my heart, we won this game."

Television replays from a variety of angles appeared to show that Davison caught the ball. However, Wiggins's "kick" was a whole other issue. Intentionally kicking the ball is a 15-yard penalty and loss of down in college football. Did Wiggins kick the ball on purpose?

"Frankly, it's very hard to see what happened to the ball," said Tigers head coach Larry Smith. "What you can see is our defensive back nails Wiggins and strips him of the ball. You see the ball going down, but you really can't see what happens after that."

"I thought I had a chance to pull it in myself, since it hadn't hit the ground yet," said Wiggins days after the game. "All I remember is it probably was a natural reaction. I fell down, and I was falling backward and my leg just went up. The ball just happened to be there, and that's what came about."

The play, also nicknamed the "Flea-Kicker," was so memorable that ESPN recognized it after the season with two ESPY

Awards, one for College Football Play of the Year and another for overall Play of the Year. The knock-down, drag-out affair, which had the teams trading punches, was so memorable that *College Football News* ranked it number 84 among its Top 100 games in college football history.

Even without the astounding turn of events, it had been an eventful game for the Tigers. By covering 78 yards in twelve plays and scoring on a 1-yard touchdown plunge by senior running back Brock Olivo, Mizzou became only the second team in 1997 to score against Nebraska on its opening drive.

Nebraska countered with 76- and 42-yard touchdown drives—capped with 16- and 1-yard touchdown runs, respectively, by Frost—to forge ahead 14–7.

Missouri tied the game on three big plays—a 48-yard kickoff return by Ricky Ross, a 28-yard pass from Corby Jones to Ricardo Rhodes, and an 18-yard touchdown pass from Jones to Torey Coleman. Ahman Green's 7-yard touchdown run put Nebraska back on top 21–14. The Tigers answered with 10 consecutive points—a 39-yard field goal and a 34-yard scoring pass from Jones to Olivo that was set up by a Shad Criss interception—to take a 24–21 halftime lead.

Frost's third rushing touchdown of the day capped a 99-yard drive and put Nebraska ahead 28–24 in the third quarter. But the Cornhuskers held the lead for just a little more than two minutes. A 62-yard kickoff return by Devin West gave Missouri great field position, and Jones's 6-yard somersault into the end zone gave the Tigers a 31–28 advantage.

The elusive Jones, who completed 12 of 20 passes for 233 yards and 3 touchdowns, pulled off miracles throughout the game. With an additional 60 rushing yards, he accounted for 293 of Missouri's 386 yards of total offense against a Nebraska defense that ranked fourth nationally.

Frost was equally dynamic, rushing for 141 and 4 touchdowns and passing for 175 yards and the game-tying score. The Tigers did have 2 interceptions, and the second one, by Harold Piersey, gave Mizzou the ball on the Nebraska 30 yard line and paved the way for the Tigers' 38–31 lead.

"I thought we were pretty well done for," Cornhuskers head coach Tom Osborne said.

"We did not give in, but we couldn't land the knockout blow," Jones said after the game. "If they're number one, then we're in the top 10."

Missouri ended fourteen consecutive losing seasons by defeating Baylor the following week and finishing the regular season at 7–4. With a 5–3 conference record that put the Tigers third overall in the Big 12 Conference standings, Mizzou earned a trip to the Holiday Bowl—its first postseason game since losing to Steve Young's Brigham Young Cougars in the 1983 Holiday Bowl.

In a Holiday Bowl shootout, the Tigers were let down by their special teams and lost 35–24 to Colorado State. Jones rushed for 132 yards and a touchdown, and West added 104 yards on 11 carries.

Getting back into bowl games was an important step for Missouri as the Tigers returned to respectability. Developing a Heisman Trophy candidate at quarterback in the multidimensional Brad Smith cemented Mizzou's re-emergence on the national scene.

Icon. Superstar. Dynamic double threat. Choir boy. Heisman and All-America candidate. Team captain. Mercurial play-

Broken Records

Tigers quarterback Brad Smith had posted some incredible personal bests and school records by the end of his third season in 2004:

Touchdowns, season: 19 (18 rush, 1 receiving, 2003)

Touchdowns rush, season: 18 (2003)

Touchdowns combined, season: 30 (18 rush, 1 receiving, 11 passing, 2003)

Touchdowns, game: 5 (Texas Tech 10/25/03)

Points, game: 30 (5 touchdowns vs. Texas Tech 10/25/03)

Rushing yards per carry, season: 6.6 (2003)

Passing attempts, season: 369 (2004)

Passing attempts, career: 1,085 (2002–04)

Passing completions, season: 211 (2003)

Touchdown passes, career: 43 (2002–04)

Total offense, season: 3,383 (1,406 rush, 1,977 pass; 2003)

Total offense, career: 9,483 (2,988 rush, 6,495 pass; 2002–04) maker. Baryshnikov in cleats. There are so many ways to describe Smith, it's nearly impossible to pick just one phrase.

Missouri head coach Gary Pinkel has described arguably the greatest player ever to wear the black and gold (at least statistically) with Boy Scout qualities—trustworthy, loyal, helpful, friendly, courteous, kind, obedient, cheerful, thrifty, brave, clean, and reverent. However, Pinkel may have offered the most accurate description of Smith when he called the Tigers' all-time leader in total offense the Gift.

In just three seasons, Smith, who returned for his senior year in 2005, has dazzled Mizzou faithful with enough exploits to last a lifetime. He started every game since his redshirt freshman season in 2002, earning honorable mention and third-team All–Big 12 honors in 2002 and 2003, respectively.

Through 2004 the honorable mention All-American had set or tied at least thirteen school records, including pass attempts (1,085) and touchdowns (19), rushing touchdowns (18), and touchdowns accounted for (18 rushing, 1 receiving, 11 passing) in a season (2003).

In just his first two seasons, Smith surpassed quarterback Jeff Handy (6,640 yards) and shattered Missouri's record for total offense in a career. As he entered his senior year in 2005, he had pushed the total to 9,483 total yards (2,988 rush, 6,495 pass). In 2003 Smith scored 118 points, placing him second on the school's single-season list behind Bob Steuber's 121 in 1942.

Not only has Smith obliterated the record book, he stands poised to break even more records. His 6,495 career passing yards and 598 completions are second all-time to Handy's 6,959 and

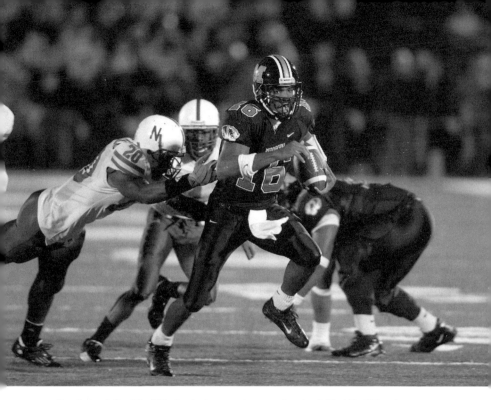

Quarterback Brad Smith's greatest moment came when he guided the Tigers to a stunning 41–24 upset of Nebraska in 2003. Newman Lawrence

618. At the end of 2004, Smith stood third among Tigers runners with 2,988 career rushing yards. Only Zach Abron (3,198 yards), and Brock Olivo (3,026) had more. Abron has the most 100-yard rushing games in Missouri history with 11, but Smith is hot on Abron's tail with 10.

"You always have to worry about Brad Smith," Colorado safety J. J. Billingsley told the *Denver Post*. "When he starts scrambling, he's dangerous."

Ironic that Smith—who was born with a foot deformity that required doctors to break his ankles and prescribe a treatment of braces, casts, and corrective shoes to fix the problem—would eventually record such gaudy numbers on a national stage. Because Smith hadn't fully matured physically and he didn't run a pass-oriented offense, recruiters from large schools stayed away from Chaney High School, which didn't even have its own field.

Pinkel, who began recruiting Smith while serving as head coach at Toledo in 2000, didn't stop his pursuit of the talented athlete when he took over at Missouri. Smith chose the Tigers over schools such as Toledo, Bowling Green, and Youngstown State.

Bishop Norman Wagner of the Mount Calvary Pentecostal Church, which served as Smith's second home during his youth in Youngstown, Ohio, gave Pinkel his blessing for recruiting Smith and then told the coach, "You have no idea what you've got here. Coach, you have no idea."

Smith, who was changing signals at the line of scrimmage for his church league team Sons of Thunder at age ten, has been an early starter all his life. And it didn't take him long to show Pinkel exactly what he had.

As a redshirt freshman in 2002, Smith started every game and eventually became only the second player in NCAA Division-I history to surpass 1,000 yards rushing and 2,000 yards passing in the same season. Clemson's Woody Dantzler, who passed for 2,360 yards and rushed for 1,004, was the first to accomplish the feat in 2001.

Smith set an NCAA record for a freshman quarterback, rushing for 1,019 yards. He ran or passed for at least 20 yards on 48 plays in 2002. In his college debut—a 33–20 victory over Illinois—Smith earned national Player of the Week honors by rushing for 138 yards.

Eight games into his freshman season, Smith broke Corby Jones's school record for total offense. At the end of the year,

How to Gage Success

One of the finest wide receivers to play football at Missouri was also a Tiger basketball star. The 6-foot 4-inch, 200-pound Justin Gage, who played forward for the Tigers and was a fifth-round draft choice of the Chicago Bears in 2003, left Missouri owning almost all of the school's receiving records. He was a four-year letterman from 1999 to 2002 and was an Associated Press All–Big 12 first-team selection his final two years (and an honorable mention in 2000).

Records

Receptions, game: 16 (Bowling Green, 2002)

Receptions, season: 82 (2002)

Receptions, career: 200

Receiving yards, game: 236 (Baylor, 2001; Bowling Green, 2002)

Receiving yards, career: 2,704

Touchdown receptions, career: 18

Consecutive games with a reception: 34

Most games with 100-plus receiving yards: 11

Justin Gage caught almost everything thrown his way as a receiver for the Tigers.

Smith was selected as the Big 12 Newcomer of the Year and Offensive Freshman of the Year.

Smith is most feared for what he can do with his feet. He led the Tigers in rushing as a freshman and sophomore, and his 1,406 rushing yards in 2003 marked the second-highest total in school history and the fourth-highest total among quarterbacks in NCAA history (Air Force quarterback Beau Morgan holds the record with 1,494). In 2003 Smith set a school record by averaging 6.6 yards per carry.

However, opponents who think Smith is just a runner find out the hard way that his arm can be just as potent. He throws extremely well on the run and is especially efficient when he rolls out or bootlegs.

In 2002 Smith set a Tigers record with 366 pass attempts. In 2004 he surpassed that mark with 369 and became the all-time leader in touchdown passes with 43. His 211 completions in 2003 are the most in Missouri history, and his 2,033 passing yards that same year are the second-most in a single season. Jeff Handy had 2,462 in 1992.

Humility is one of the traits that makes Smith truly exceptional. In 1994 he and All–Big 12 center A. J. Ricker were driving from Columbia to a Fellowship of Christian Athletes meeting in Kansas City. Smith looked up to watch a stealth bomber, and when he looked down he noticed he was speeding. So did a Missouri state highway patrolman.

According to Ricker, he told Smith to tell the patrolman he was the Missouri quarterback. Smith politely declined and accepted the ticket without trying to receive preferential treatment.

"Of all the things that make me, football is just a part of that—and a small part," Smith told the *Kansas City Star*. "God didn't make us like that, to have football number one and Him last. You'll never be successful that way. Football, you can get hurt. Your career ends after a while. If that's all you base your life on, you'll have a mental breakdown. I put more focus on my family and what's really going to matter in the long run, how I live my life."

Smith gets the royal treatment from opponents who have constructed their defensive game plans with the primary goal of stopping the dynamic double threat. Fortunately for Mizzou fans, those strategies haven't been very successful.

One game in particular demonstrates how dangerous Smith can be. In a 62–31 victory over Texas Tech in 2003, the 6-foot 2-inch, 210-pounder put on an amazing show.

Smith rushed for 291 yards, the best rushing day of anyone in NCAA Division-I that season and the second most in a game in Tigers history. He earned national player of the week honors from almost every major sports news outlet in the country. Only Stacey Robinson of Northern Illinois (308 rushing yards against Fresno State in 1990) and Nolan Cromwell of Kansas (294 versus Oregon State in 1975) have posted a higher rushing total among quarterbacks in college history.

Smith also set school records in the Texas Tech game for the most points (30) and touchdowns (5) in a single game. His final score came on a 61-yard touchdown run.

"When he gets out he doesn't look to check it down, he goes for the jugular," said former NFL defensive coordinator and University of Texas co-defensive coordinator Greg Robinson (now the head coach at Syracuse). "You look at John Elway, you look at

Mark Brunell, you look at Brett Favre. Those are the biggest names to me that when they scramble, they're looking to throw. They're looking to gun you down. This guy does that."

Smith played a big role in one of the most memorable games in Tigers history in his sophomore season. The 1980 U.S. Olympic hockey team upset of the Soviets may have garnered greater national attention, but ask anyone in good Ol' Mizzou what the greatest upset ever is, and you'll get a resounding "The Tigers' 41–24 victory over Nebraska in 2003."

Few rivalries have ever become as lopsided as the Nebraska-Missouri battles on the football field. Dating to November 18, 1978, the Tigers had lost twenty-four consecutive games to the Cornhuskers, including the ignominious 45–38 overtime loss in Columbia in which Nebraska's Shevin Wiggins kicked a pass to another teammate for the tying touchdown that sent the game into overtime.

During Nebraska's run of dominance over Missouri, the Tigers were outscored by more than 57 points twice and by more than 42 points six times. Eleven of the losses were nationally televised. The Cornhuskers pounded the Tigers on the ground, through the air, and on special teams.

And if facing Nebraska wasn't enough of a mountain to climb, the last time the Tigers had beaten a top-10 nationally ranked team at home was a 9–0 decision over Arizona State (ranked seventh) on September 28, 1974. Since defeating ninth-ranked Mississippi State in Jackson, Mississippi, on October 3, 1981, the Tigers had lost forty-five consecutive games to teams ranked in the top ten. In fact, Missouri's last victory over a team ranked in the top twenty-five was a 51–50 double-overtime win against twelfth-ranked Oklahoma State in 1997.

Tigers head coach Gary Pinkel
brought his winning ways and
eye for talent to the Mizzou
football program.

Despite the dire forecast of another Nebraska husking of the Tigers, a crowd of 68,349—the first home sellout in four years—braved equally formidable driving rain to see if 2003 would be the year the streak stopped. Missouri was in an especially foul mood entering the game, having lost to archrival Kansas a week earlier.

The game started like so many of the previous twenty-four losses. Missouri moved the ball to Nebraska's 43 yard line on its first series, only to have freshman quarterback Brad Smith throw an interception to Nebraska safety Josh Bullocks. On the ensuing Cornhusker series, Jammal Lord tossed a swing pass to Mark LeFlore, who raced 55 yards for the game's first score.

Missouri was forced to punt on the next series, but the Tigers caught a break when Josh Davis fumbled the punt at Nebraska's 6 yard line. Two plays later, Tigers running back Zach Abron, who would rush for 84 yards on the day, tied the game with a touchdown run.

On the ensuing kickoff, Cornhusker Jim O'Halleran fumbled and Missouri recovered. Smith returned the favor by throwing an interception six plays later. However, the MU defense held, and then the Tigers opened their bag of tricks.

After receiving a lateral, wide receiver Darius Outlaw tossed a 47-yard touchdown pass to quarterback Smith. Stunningly, Mizzou had a 14–7 lead. Nebraska kicked a field goal right before halftime and scored 14 unanswered points to take a 24–14 lead through three quarters.

Missouri refused to fold. On the first play of the third quarter, Smith, who led all runners with 123 yards on 18 carries, sprinted 39 yards for a touchdown. Lord fumbled on Nebraska's next series, Missouri recovered, and that set the stage for the game-turning play.

"I thought we had gathered the momentum when we went up 10," said Cornhuskers coach Frank Solich. "We were moving the ball offensively and we were making enough plays on the defensive side of it to control. But the momentum moved back to their side. They capitalized on it."

Trailing 24–21, the Tigers moved the ball to Nebraska's 15 yard line, but their drive stalled. Missouri lined up for a 32-yard field goal attempt, but holder Sony Riccio grabbed the snap and, instead of placing down the ball, tossed a 15-yard touchdown pass to Victor Sesay.

"I felt we hadn't beat those guys in twenty-five years and we were going to be aggressive," said Tigers head coach Gary Pinkel after the game. "We talked about on fourth-and-one going for it and doing some reverses, throwback screen passes. We felt we had to do some of those things."

Smith added touchdown runs of 1 and 9 yards on Missouri's next two possessions, and the Tigers outscored Nebraska 27–0 in the fourth quarter to seal the victory.

Nebraska's offense committed five turnovers, and its defense, which entered the game as the nation's top unit, allowing only 219 yards per game, surrendered 452. The Tigers scored more points in the fourth quarter than Nebraska had given up in a game all year.

Smith tied a school record by scoring four touchdowns (three rushing and one receiving) in a game. Four others in MU history have equaled that feat (Earl Grant versus Kansas, 1978; James Wilder versus Nebraska, 1978; Marlon Adler against Iowa State,

1983; and Joe Freeman against Marshall, 1992). Smith also was the only runner to rush for more than 100 yards against Nebraska all season.

"We were able to run draws and counter plays with Brad," said Pinkel. "I told Brad just to turn it loose. With his athleticism, if you feel you're on eggshells, you have to watch yourself on everything you do. Then you can't use your athleticism."

Despite being soaked by the rain, no Tigers fans left the stadium early. When they did finally leave their seats, it was to tear down both goal posts after the game.

"I've told some people that our program will eventually beat some people," said Pinkel. "I was getting tired. I was really frustrated because I'm not very patient. But it's nice to get this first one."

About the Author

Brian C. Peterson has covered football as a writer and editor for the National Football League for the past fifteen years and has bled the black and gold of Missouri football since 1987. A former scholarship linebacker at Azusa Pacific University and walk-on defensive back at Mizzou, Peterson brings a wealth of football expertise and a passion for the sport to all of his projects, which include hundreds of feature stories in magazines, newspapers, and on the Internet; radio commentary; and three books (*Terrell Davis, 1001 Facts About Running Backs,* and *NFL Rules! Bloopers, Pranks, Upsets, and Touchdowns*).